Praises for Chosen:

With a likeness to John Bunyan's, The Pilgrim's Progress, **Chosen** will take you on a metaphorical journey as you embark on an exhilarating pilgrimage side by side with the Redeemer. With creative writing that will capture your imagination, and enlighten your soul, **Chosen** invites your senses to come alive as you experience the constant presence of Love and Spirit, and glean wisdom from Peace, Lesson, and Kindness. Through mountaintops and valleys, each page will prick your heart with truth and grace and will overwhelm you with the encompassing reality that Jesus indeed calls you Chosen! *Chosen* is an invitation to commune with your Redeemer and understand His love for you. Are you ready to embark on this journey with Him?
—**Emily Elizabeth Anderson**, Thriving Forward Ministries.

***

As a therapist, I know all too well that our perspectives are shaped by our lives in this world. Because of this, experiences and interactions leave each of us with very unique perceptions of ourselves, the world around us, and our futures. If we have been hurt, abandoned, or rejected in any way, we tend to layer that pain and understanding (or misunderstanding) onto our perception of God too. This can leave us further damaged, and even very misled at times in our spiritual walk. Anna's allegorical approach to writing this book has the potential to draw you in as a reader and pull you into a journey to understand more fully

Chosen

who our Redeemer actually is to us. Ask the Holy Spirit to guide you as you read, and to stretch you and your understanding of the Triune God. As you explore a fresh perspective of our Redeemer, be prepared to question why you hold the beliefs you do about who He is and how He relates to us. I am always amazed when He begins to reveal layer after layer of His personality and desires for us.

—Keri Kitchen, MED, LPCC, NCC; Faith & Focus Coach; The Every Day Royalty Podcast.

***

Chosen is a whimsical piece of writing saturated with emotion and intimacy. A visual feast that speaks to our deepest insecurities and struggles, with reminders of hope, redemption, and love. It is an adventure in imagination, with Scripture as its guide. Every character and place in this story has a purpose, and you quickly dive headfirst into the experience. I was struck by so many teachable moments etched throughout this story. I think this will be a great tool for sharing the truth of the Gospel to many who wouldn't otherwise give it a chance. But it's also a refreshing take for those of us who have been on the journey for a long time, to experience the Gospel in a new way. The result is a beautiful self-examination of the heart, peeled back delicately with every page. It is also an exquisite reminder of who the Redeemer is, and all that He has for you.

—Jeanette Brown, Jeanette and Her Stages.

***

Love comes in all shapes and in all sizes. Love blossoms in the morning as the sun rays touch the petals of a tulip or a rose as it opens up in all of its splendor and beauty. Love comes at the sound of a bird chirping outside of your window in the early mornings. Or the sound of the wind blowing through the trees. Love comes at the first sound of the cry of a newborn baby after a long nine months

Chosen

wait, that was full of hope and anticipation. Love also comes from the words that are written on the pages of Anna's book, ***Chosen***. Words that are penned from her heart by the Holy Spirit to uplift, inspire, encourage & to bring hope and joy as we go on our journey with the Lord. The word of the Lord teaches us in Matthew 22:14 that many have been called, but few are chosen. Anna was chosen.
—**Annie T. Broughton**, Founder & Talk Show Host of "Just Call Me Sarah."

***

Anna does a great job displaying the different biblical aspects in an engaging way. This short but powerful book has the potential to touch lives for eternity. As it opens the eyes of our hearts to receive a new measure of intimacy with Jesus. It also helps us grasp just how much we are loved by our Heavenly Father.
—**Jennifer Elston**, Pastor; Conference Speaker.

***

Anna Pranger never ceases to amaze me. Her heart for people to experience Jesus is contagious and welcoming. The title of this book alone should draw you into the fact that Jesus is calling you to something. I love how Anna has used the question "Who is Chosen?" to show us grace for what we might face daily. Sometimes the truth is really hard to believe when all we see is what we are going through. Maybe you feel guilt, shame or some kind of pain that tells you that you are not enough. Maybe you've been told you are not enough. I love the truth, not only because it sets me free from these beliefs BUT because it also shows me that God can use anyone. If you picked up this book and were desiring a journey, get ready for the ride! Get ready to be challenged & shown that you are chosen.
—**Grace Graber**, Artist; Singer, songwriter.

CHOSEN

A Journey of Victory with Jesus Your Savior

Anna Pranger

Published by KHARIS PUBLISHING, imprint of KHARIS MEDIA LLC.

Copyright © 2021 Anna Pranger

ISBN-13: 978-1-63746-104-4

ISBN-10: 1-63746-104-6

Library of Congress Control Number: 2021950852

All rights reserved. This book or parts thereof may not be reproduced in any form, stored in a retrieval system, or transmitted in any form by any means - electronic, mechanical, photocopy, recording, or otherwise - without prior written permission of the publisher, except as provided by United States of America copyright law.

All Scripture quotations, unless otherwise indicated, are taken from the Holy Bible, English Standard Version ®, ESV®. Copyright © 2001 by Crossway, a publishing ministry of Good News Publishers. Used by permission. All rights reserved.

All KHARIS PUBLISHING products are available at special quantity discounts for bulk purchase for sales promotions, premiums, fund-raising, and educational needs. For details, contact:

Kharis Media LLC
Tel: 1-479-599-8657
support@kharispublishing.com
www.kharispublishing.com

Acknowledgement

I want to thank my parents for their continued love and support as they encouraged me on this journey. They have been a true support and encouragement this past season.

I want to dedicate this book to my Grandpa Joe. He taught me about the power of abiding in Jesus and walking daily with Him. His life impacted countless people as He truly embodied the meaning of 'being the hands and feet of Jesus.' Forever in my heart Grandpa, until we meet again!

May we never forget to display the love of Jesus and in all that we do for as long as we are given here on earth.

TABLE OF CONTENTS

	Prologue	xi
1	The Redeemer	1
2	A Waltz Through Time	5
3	It's Time to Soar	9
4	A Heart that Hungers	15
5	Power of the Mind	21
6	Shield of Faith	29
7	One More Step	36
8	In the Boat	43
9	Helmet of Salvation	49
10	Kindness of Redeemer	55
11	The Cross	64
	Chosen – Study Guide: Soul Expression	72
	New Book Coming Soon….	131

Prologue

Welcome back to the journey you initially began with Love; as you embraced your identity and learned your purpose and calling. God desires a real and intimate relationship with you. I pray that is exactly what you found on your journey of "Loved." I want more for you though, there is a savior that knows you by name and understands what you have faced. He knows all about temptations and living in a cruel world. Before we continue though, it is important that you remember that Jesus only did what He heard the Father say. The groundwork that was laid for your understanding of peace, trials, and the love of God is what we are building on. We are here to discover who Redemption is and why He calls us chosen. As we address the idols that hold of back from living in a position of authority and truly seeing ourselves the way Jesus sees us; we must remember that Jesus to was tempted, but He never sinned. Together we are going to learn how Jesus overcame and what following in His footsteps as overcomers entails.

Before we can discuss who, Redemption is, we must first understand who originated the idea of Redemption. We can find our answer in John 3:16 "For God so loved the world, that he gave his only Son, that whoever believes in him should not perish but have eternal life." God's desire for you is eternal life with Him, and Jesus made that possible through His blood and sacrifice. So, if

Prologue

you want to truly understand Redemption, look up, He is smiling down at you.

What is Redemption? Can it be defined as a single act of kindness? This is a simple yet profound question we must ask ourselves as we examine what it means to define our Redeemer. In my previous book, *Loved*, we experienced the story of Love as we read about a creator who painted the sky and called us by name. What about our Redeemer though? The One who is infinite and one with the Trinity? The Spirit who became flesh only to experience struggle and pain? A God made flesh and incarnate-- the true solution to defeating evil? A man who was tempted, beaten, belittled, and broken, yet did not sin? A standard has been set, as the red letters in the bible teach us the ways of a God who became man for our Redemption. What is this kind of love? What if this is truly the love, we have all been searching for? The peace that fills our soul. The words written on our hearts, so we know we were worth dying for. Can you muster an ounce of faith to pause, reflect, and believe that a perfect God could sympathize with a sin-natured soul, and not just sympathize but redeem that soul? God has a perfect plan to take you from broken to whole; from sick to healthy; sinful to wanted. This plan takes a soul that is hell-bound and calls it to the golden gates of eternity. Slave to child and, even more so, *chosen child*.

Don't let other people's opinions of the Redeemer stop you from discovering who He is for yourself. Because when you lock eyes with Jesus, everything changes. He is the Way, the Truth, and the Life, and the only way to the Father of eternity is through a relationship with Him. Put your bias and doubts aside and let me tell you about my

Jesus. The One who knows how you feel; the One who has seen Hell itself and laughed in the enemy's face as He defeated him for once and for all. The One who is on your side interceding on your behalf. He *gets* you; He *sees* you. He is on your side, cheering for you every step of the way.

The world filled with its brokenness may try to sway your opinion of Jesus; but once you experience the word that became flesh, you will never be swayed by faithlessness again. Put on your armor, remember your journey with Love, and with open arms embrace the Redeemer of your soul.

Chapter One

The Redeemer

While we wait for the blessed hope—the appearing of the glory of our great God and Savior, Jesus Christ, who gave himself for us to redeem us from all wickedness and to purify for himself a people that are his very own, eager to do what is good. - Titus 2:13-14

Hello, my friend. My eyes dance with color as I look into your eyes, and my Spirit is wild about you. Allow me to introduce myself: I Am Redeemer, the very embodiment of Redemption. I was chosen by my Father to take the place of pain so you would not have to do so. My Spirit is one with the Father's, and my mind is set on the things above. When I was in the world, I was not moved by the things of the world. I know the temptations of sin, as I too was once tempted. I have seen what pride does to a man, as I once called out sin through stories of long ago. I Am alive and real. Stories of me have been told throughout the pages of history; they were not fairytales as one may suppose; they were real.

I came to redeem the world and set the example for the life I have called you to live; my example is your roadmap. We are not as different as you may think. In fact, our DNA crosses through time as we are both called a child of God. My love for you is deep and wide like that of my Father's, and I understand your struggles and pain as I, too, cried out to Father to deliver me from pain. Friend, I

The Redeemer

became flesh so that what sin has stolen can be reclaimed. What was once missing--relationship with God--is now found once again through my sacrifice. I crossed the barrier so you can commune with Father. Sin has been defeated and death has been reclaimed. I have come to give you life--and life more abundantly. I was the first and I am the last. Through union with me, you too will discover what it means to be set apart. The sin in this world hated me; it too will hate you. But friend, it will be worth it.

Apart from anything else, I ask that you remove your walls that you have set against me and allow my kindness to crawl into your heart. I know the world has left you dry and defeated. I know you have been rejected. My friend, I know this because the world rejected me, too. My love is not tainted; in fact, I died for those who rejected me. I gave my life for those who spit in my face, and I would do it all over again. My blood was spilled on your behalf and has the power to set you free from your pain and tormenting thoughts. It also has the power to replace what was lost as you find the answers you long for.

I am kind, patient, and good. I am also filled with joy. I want to add some joy back to your life as you dream and imagine with me. I will add passion to your life as I transform your dry heart to one heaping with compassion. My word outlines my desire to walk with you as I disciple you in the ways of my strategic wisdom. Break me out of the box you have put me in, Friend, as I have much to show you.

Let's continue on the journey that you started with Love not that long ago. In my presence there is no man-made time, just a union of richness to be explored. Let us journey into your imagination where creativity lives and where I come alive. I won't fail or hurt you; with your hand in mine, you are safe. Allow your smile to fill your face as the colors of my personality give life to your dry bones.

Hear the words as I speak to them out loud: "I choose you; I choose past, present, and future you. I will never stop choosing you. You are Chosen." Now follow me.

You are pulled through the darkness and into the light as your eyes slowly adjust to the brightness. You take in the view and realize you are once again standing on the mountaintop filled with trees and lush grass. You make long strides to the edge and peer into the familiar canyon below. The canyon rocks are a reddish color, and you gaze up at the grass lining the side of the mountain peak. You look down at your feet and see they are fitted with the shoes of the gospel of Peace. You shriek, "I AM BACK," as you bring your hand to your chest and feel the hard armor of the breastplate of Righteousness.

You leap in the air allowing your body to soar for a few seconds. You feel the cool breeze of Wind joyfully wrap and unwrap your body in an embrace. Your gaze takes in the blue sky, and you watch as a bird soars overhead. The mountain ridge catches your gaze as you let your eyes trail in the distance. Your eyes settle on two forms sitting off in the distance; they appear to be chatting intensely as their legs dangle off the side of the cliff.

You make your way to them, catching their unfamiliar chatter. As you approach the back of the two forms, you instantly recognize Love. Your heart leaps as you watch Love's white hair blow in the wind. His strong shoulders are poised perfectly as His white robe shines with brilliance. You are overcome with glory as you gaze upon the back of the One whom you love. You watch as His head slowly turns in your direction and His fire filled eyes meet yours. A giant smile spreads across His face.

"CHILD, I am so glad you are back."

The words are a melody to your ears as a wide smile spreads across your face. Wind blows lightly moving the lush grass back and forth. Love turns to the man next to Him and whispers something in His ear. The man nods excitedly, stands, and turns in your direction. His eyes stare into yours, and He gives a wink. Your heart leaps as you recognize His calm face and tranquil demeanor.

"Redeemer," you gasp as you take a tentative step back. Suddenly the image of the Acacia Tree fills your memory as you remember Redeemer standing tall with a sword in hand. Redeemer walks past you, and your eyes follow Him until He is out of sight. You bring your attention back to Love who stands and walks in your direction. "Why is Redeemer here?" you question as Love excitedly grabs your hand and twirls you around. "Oh, you will see, but for now, let's dance," He exclaims with an excitement that makes you giddy.

Chapter Two

A Waltz Through Time

You have turned my mourning into dancing; You have loosed my sackcloth and girded me with gladness. - Psalm 30:11

Hand in Hand with Love, He pulls you close. The air on the mountaintop is cool as the setting sun gives a purple glow to your grassy dance floor. Love steps forward with his left foot. You step back with your right. Memories of the broken chains deep in the canyon cross your mind. You look into Love's eyes and feel your heart swell with thankfulness.

Love steps to the right with his right foot. You step to the left with your left foot. You gaze into Love's eyes until He twirls you. Within the twirl you see the memories of The Cactus and how Love rescued you from your rejection and tore down your walls.

Love catches your hand as you come out of the twirl and closes His left foot to his right. You follow suit by closing your right foot to your left. You lean your head back as Wind blows the sweet aroma of honey through the air bringing to mind the renewal of The Acacia Tree.

Love steps back with his right foot. You step forward with your left foot. With the moving of your foot, you are reminded of the steps taken in the desert and how you almost gave up completely, only to find Love chasing you down and rescuing you from *you*. The cool breeze continues to blow.

Love steps to the left with His left foot. You step to the right with your right foot. You gaze down at His hand holding yours as the memories of creation singing "Holy, Holy, Holy" fill your mind. The words are music to your ears; tears fill your eyes as His holy presence closes in.

Love closes his right foot to His left. You instinctively close your left foot to the right. You gaze into Love's eyes as you remember the war scene and how Love rescued every single person along with Wind, an...and your mind grasps to remember, and "Redeemer" Love finishes your thought.

The grass is cool beneath your feet as He twirls you and then pulls you close into His embrace.

"The time has come to journey with the lamb who was slain on your behalf."

Confused, you gaze into His eyes longing to stay in His arms.

"I am always near and never far," Love says assuredly, "but it's time to journey with my Son."

Wind blows harder as Love spins you outward. He lets go of your hand and you twirl straight into the arms of Redeemer.

Redeemer catches your hand with ease, as a bright smile spreads across His face. You bring your other hand to His as you fall into step with Him. The sun slowly disappears behind the mountain leaving a deep purple hue.

Chosen

Wind lightly whips within your step. You fall into step with Redeemer as the waltz continues.

Redeemer steps forward with his left foot. You step back with your right. You gaze at Him as you take in His structured face and piercing eyes surrounded by laugh lines.

Redeemer steps to the right with his right foot. You step to the left with your left foot. You bring your gaze to His lips hiding beneath His bushy beard. He twirls you around and catches your hand as you come out of the twirl. Your trust in Him grows.

He closes His left foot to His right. You follow suit by closing your right foot to your left. Your gaze climbs to the top of His head as His hair moves in the wind.

Redeemer steps back with his right foot. You step forward with your left foot. Your gaze finally settles into His eyes as you look into them deeply. His smile shines through His eyes as His laugh lines crease. A rainbow of color display in His eyes and then settles to a still fire. Entrenched in His gaze, Redeemer closes his right foot to His left. You instinctively close your left foot to your right.

Redeemer releases your hand and takes a low bow. The moon shines a glow on the grassy dance floor as the stars shine far overhead. The crickets hum and the grass blows as the mountain peaks glisten in the darkness of the night. Redeemer stands and you give a gentle bow in His direction. You bring your body back upright and gaze into the eyes of Redeemer as the corner of your lips break into a smile. Redeemer begins to laugh, and you match His tone with your own laughter. You plop to the ground overcome by laughter. Redeemer finds a spot next to you as the sound of His laughter continues. You gasp for breath as you calm your laughing body. Your eyes find Redeemer; He is still, with a joyful smile on His face.

You take a deep breath and move closer to Him. You stare out above the mountaintops and up to the stars. You allow your body to relax as you lie down on your back and gaze at the stars. You hear Redeemer shifting as His body falls next to yours. He reaches for your hand placed comfortably at your side and wraps His hand around yours.

"I am so excited to begin this journey with you, my chosen friend."

The words bring warmth to your heart as joyful tears fall from your eyes.

You squeeze Redeemer's hand three times to say, "I love you," and rest your head on His shoulder. "When I first met you on my journey with Love, I thought you were stern as you claimed, "the blood is enough" with a sword in hand, but now I can see you are kind and similar to Love."

Redeemer stays still for a moment, then replies, "I am stern when I talk about the blood that was shed, and soon you will learn why. But for now, you must know that I Am who I Am and my kindness is what draws my friends close to me." His words bring you comfort as your body sinks heavily against the ground, and you fall into a deep slumber.

Chapter Three

It's Time to Soar

But you would be fed with the finest of wheat; with honey from the rock, I would satisfy you. - Psalm 81:16

A sweet aroma fills your nostrils. You open your eyes as the sun clears the mountaintop displaying an array of unique colors. You sit up and inhale deeply; the sweet smell engulfs the air. *Honey*--the thought fills your mind as you wrap your arms around your legs snugly. You stretch your neck to your right and then left and let out a light yawn as you bask in the feeling of freshness from a complete night's sleep. You bring your eyes from the sunrise and find Redeemer squatted next to a campfire with a skillet in His hand. You move your hands tight across your chest as you stand and begin to take a light step towards Him. His gaze meets yours as He looks up from the skillet; a bright smile spreads across His face.

"Ahhh, good morning, friend."

The words are sweet to your ears as you smile in His direction. He pats the ground and motions for you to sit next to Him. You walk gingerly to Him and sit.

Your gaze is mesmerized by the campfire as colors of blue, red, and orange dance before you. You close your eyes and breathe in the sweet honey aroma. The sun grows warm on your face as the morning campfire crackles lightly. You open your eyes and gaze up at Redeemer's strong face. His concentration is fixed solely on the skillet.

"What are you making?" you whisper.

A bright smile spreads across His face as His eyes meet yours dancing with mischief.

"Taste and see," He says with a teasing tone.

With the flick of His wrist, a gooey pancake soars through the air landing perfectly into the skillet. Redeemer reaches to His side for a tin plate and flops the pancake from the skillet onto the plate. He smiles widely as He hands the plate to you.

You take the plate from His hands and stare down intently at the perfect pancake placed on your plate. Honey begins to ooze out of the side and the top forcing the pancake to crack from the center. The smell of honey causes your mouth to water, and you brush your finger against the honey and bring it to your lips. The taste is sweet and warm. The texture is smooth. You lick your lips as the feeling of warm honey slides into your belly.

Your eyes widen as you exclaim, "WHAT IS THIS?"

A satisfied laugh leaves Redeemer's throat as He leans His head back and lets out another chuckle.

"It's breakfast," He says between chuckles.

You brush your finger against the pancake, this time breaking it. The honey oozes out, and you dip the broken piece of pancake in the honey and bring the warm pancake to your lips and savor the bite as it slips down your throat. One bite turns to two as you savor each one until the honey filled pancake is gone. Redeemer reaches for your plate with a smile and places it next to His side. He brings His finger to a rock surrounding the campfire and gently taps it. To your amazement, rich water begins to gush out. Instinctively you cup your hands and reach into the water and bring it to your mouth. The richness of the water cleanses your parched mouth as you drink it in.

"Living water!"

You gaze up at Redeemer as the words hit your ears. He stands and gives you a slight wink.

"It's time to go," He says kindly, as you stand and brush the water from your hands. "Where are we going?" you ask with excitement.

"On an adventure," He replies.

Redeemer reaches for your hand and you grasp it. His steps turn into a slight jog and then into a run. He lets go of your hand and takes the lead. You race after Him.

You match His pace as you run along the mountaintop; the wind blows quickly through your hair; a smile is plastered on your face. With your eyes wide open you take in the view of the mountaintops glistening in the midday sun. You gaze down at your feet as they pound in a rhythm across the rocks. Your eyes look to Redeemer's feet running steadily as He quickens just two steps ahead of you. You trace His legs and stature and find His face beaming with delight as He stares out into the distance. Your gaze matches His, and you are overcome with fear as you run straight towards the ledge of the canyon.

You reach for Redeemer's hand, but it's too late. You feel your body lift off the ground as you clear the ledge

It's Time to Soar

and freefall through the air. You begin to flail your arms as you catch the wind. A scream climbs through your throat as you choke on the air. The sensation of falling leaps into your bones.

"JUST SOAR!" The words come crashing into your mind as you hear the voice of Wind.

You reach out your arms and a feeling of comfort hovers over you. Suddenly you stop falling and look over to find Redeemer clutching your hand, causing your body to float in place. His smile is wide, and He begins to laugh. Your body calms under the sound, and you begin to laugh too as Wind fills your lungs with fresh air.

"Friend, it's time to soar."

Your eyes hear the words roll off Redeemer's tongue. You loosen your rigid body and let go of Redeemer's hand. You flap your arms like a bird and straighten them as you soar through the canyon. Redeemer races out in front of you. As your confidence grows, you pick up speed and glide through the sides of the canyon. You gaze down below and every rock and ridge appear tiny. You turn to the left and right and allow your body to spin in a spiral and roll into a flip.

"That's it, move with Wind," Redeemer yells as He spins around and flips backward.

After another flip and spiral, you follow Redeemer as you brush against the side of the canyon. Another flip and you watch as Redeemer enters into a nosedive. You follow closely as you head straight for the ground. The wind blows heavy against your face as you near the trees below. You watch Redeemer straighten out His body and land on the ground perfectly. With your sight on Redeemer, you bring your head back up as you even out your body then give a few more flaps of your arms as your feet lightly touch the ground. You step onto the ground in a running motion as your arms find your side. You run straight into Redeemer's open arms, laughing, while the speed from running knocks you both over.

You hit the ground with ease and roll onto your back laughing. Loud laughter comes from Redeemer as He holds His belly and rolls to His side. Your gaze meets His, and His eyes sparkle with colors of delight. Your laughter slows to a chuckle then a smile as you roll to your side and gaze deeper into His eyes.

"That was the most exhilarating thing I have ever done."

Redeemer smiles, "That is what letting go feels like."

The words cut deep into your soul as you roll onto your back and stare up at the fluffy white clouds forming in the light blue sky.

"I hope I keep letting go then." The words leave your mouth in a whisper.

Redeemer brings His hand to your head and strokes your hair softly. "That's your next adventure, Chosen Friend--the adventure of letting go."

The words sound smooth like honey as the memory of the honey pancake fills your mind. "So the journey is sweet then?" You ask the question in a hopeful manner. "Ahh yes, friend, the journey is sweet, but it will also crack you open and expose what is on the inside."

It's Time to Soar

Your brow furrows with frustration as you sit up and stare out into the distance. Redeemer gently sits up and gazes at your face. He reaches for your hand slowly and grips it tightly. You squeeze His hand back, and a gentle tear falls from your face as you turn your head to meet His gaze.

"It's easy to trust you when the journey is sweet but knowing that I will be cracked open makes it hard."

Redeemer moves His finger to your cheek and catches your tear. "I felt the same when I cried out in the garden for the cup to be taken from me." Redeemer moves His gaze to the ground in memory. "My Father is gracious and, much like the honey, His words and His ways are healing to the soul and to the bones."

Redeemer moves His hand to your heart. Your heart beats hard inside your chest.

"I know the journey of trust must be taken and I am ready to soar." The words slip off of your lips as you move your hand on top of Redeemer's.

A smile perks at the corner of your lips. Then the ground begins to shake, and you whip your head away from Redeemer and stare at the canyon in front of you. The shaking causes the canyon to split down the middle. Straight down where the canyon parted, a long dark forest appears. The shaking comes to a halt. Redeemer moves His hand from your heart and stands. He reaches down and you grab His hand as He lifts you to your feet.

"Well then, let's go!" A smile widens across His face as He steps in the direction of the forest.

Chapter Four

A Heart that Hungers

Then Jesus was led by the Spirit into the wilderness to be tempted by the devil. After fasting forty days and forty nights, he was hungry. The tempter came to him and said, "If you are the Son of God, tell these stones to become bread." Jesus answered, "It is written: 'Man shall not live on bread alone, but on every word that comes from the mouth of God.'" - Matthew 4:1-4

Following quietly behind Redeemer, you find yourself caught in deep thought as the forest grows closer in sight, the birds chirp above, and the sun is heavy in the sky as beams of light cause sweat to form on your forehead. You wipe your brow and watch as Redeemer walks eagerly into the forest. The shade is welcoming from the heat of the sun; the forest is dense with a tiny path before you; the trees are tall and the leaves thickset. You take a step forward and a branch cracks under your feet startling you. You reach your hand to your breastplate of Righteousness and feel the beating of your heart underneath. You begin to whisper sweet melodies to yourself to calm your fearful heart.

Redeemer turns His head slowly and catches your fearful eyes. His face is calm but stern.

"Do not fear." The words are crisp as they leave His lips.

A Heart that Hungers

You nod quickly as you adjust your speed to match His. You instinctively reach for His hand, and He grasps your hand tightly.

Another branch cracks beneath your feet; the leaves begin to rustle in the wind; a crack shoots through the leaves causing flocks of birds to squawk and fly through the trees. You hit your knees as the noise of the flapping birds startle your already fearful heart. Redeemer reaches down His hand and strokes your face lightly.

"Friend, you must trust the process; this is the journey to fullness."

Your heart quakes at the sound of His words. Unable to speak, you stand and nod again. Redeemer takes a few steps forward and you follow Him closely as the leaves continue to blow. Your eyes catch a clearing up ahead. Redeemer quickens His steps and reaches the clearing. You follow closely. He suddenly stops in the middle of the clearing. The trees surround the clearing in a perfect circle, and in the middle under your feet is soft grass. The sun grows heavy on your face as you close your eyes and tilt your head to the sky. Your heavy breathing slows, and the heat feels good to your fearful heart. You bring your head back down and your eyes find Redeemer. Your heart leaps at the sight of His beautiful smile. He stops walking then sits slowly and motions for you to join Him.

You sit next to Him and place your hands at your side as you run the soft grass through your fingers. Redeemer reaches to His right and encases a wood tablet in His hands. He brings His face to the surface of the wood and gives a gentle blow as dust particles invade the air. He brushes off the remaining dust, and His fingertips brush

Chosen

lightly against the forming words. He gazes upon the wood; His face changes from joy to discontentment. You study His face as He grows more concerned. His brow furrows and His eyes narrow; mist fills His eyes as He gazes deeply at the wood tablet in His hand.

Your questioning gaze stares impatiently as you inch closer to see what He sees. Redeemer's sharp gaze catches your own and you lunge back. His eyes, soft but stern, burn into yours. Your heart begins to pound as He offers the wood to you. With shaky hands you grasp the wood tablet and bring it to your eyes. Your eyes wander from line to line as each word is perfectly depicted. The pounding of your heart lessens as you read each line, and pride swells there instead as the memories of the words replay in your mind.

The wind begins to blow as the sun disappears behind a cloud. Your gaze finds Redeemer. You watch as He tilts His face to the sky and closes His eyes.

"I don't understand," you manage to whimper.

He tilts His face down and catches your expression.

He responds with a disappointed smile, "What don't you understand?"

You hold up the wood tablet inches from His face. "The words on this are my accomplishments; they are my most proud moments; they are the things I did for you." Tears fall from your eyes as you let out the last sentence.

Redeemer strokes the tear from your face and takes the wood tablet from your hand and lays it at His side. He stands and brushes the dirt from His lap and extends His hand to you.

"I want to show you something."

Confused and angry you reluctantly take His hand as He lifts you off the ground. Redeemer walks from the clearing and into the wilderness; you follow closely.

"I once walked the earth like you do. I, too, was tempted." The words come from the position of a wise father and intrigued; you lean in as you walk closer behind Him not wanting to miss a word.

"I went without food for 40 days; I was hungry and tired. The tempter came to me and questioned my divine origin, tempting me to turn a stone into bread to fill my belly."

Redeemer suddenly stops walking and turns sharply and looks deep into your eyes. The wind blows through the dense trees.

"But we do not live on bread alone, true satisfaction is found in the words of my Father."

Redeemer's breath grows heavy. Your heart begins to pound as the weight of His words shake you to your core. He turns and continues walking through the forest.

"You don't hunger for bread though, you hunger for satisfaction, you hunger for accomplishments, you hunger for idols, you hunger for these things more than you hunger for me."

The words feel like a shot of lightning as you fall to your knees; the sobs come from your core and spill out from deep inside of you.

Chosen

The trees rustle heavily as the cracks of breaking sticks beneath your knees match the breaking of your heart. Your body shakes under the weight of the words that appear once again: your accomplishments, your most proud moments, and the things you did in His name but without Him.

"I am so sorry," you mutter between sobs, "everything I do, I do to benefit me, to take me further, to make me look good, even the things I do in your name."

Your tears flow heavier from your eyes soaking the earth beneath you. Out of the corner of your eye, you see Redeemer move back in the center of the grass. He picks up the wood tablet that contains an inscription. You place your hands in the wet soil, push your weight to your heels, and wipe the tears from your eyes as your sobs subside. You watch as Redeemer returns to your side and kneels in front of you.

Redeemer tilts your chin up. "Look at me."

You bring your eyes to His as you feel tears form once again.

"I forgive you." He strokes your cheek as the words dance off His lips.

He holds the wood tablet out in front of you. You see a feather drawn over the top of the words. You lean back and meet His eyes.

"Repentance is my goodness."

A gentle breeze whips around your face; you close your eyes as the sound of an eagle squawks in the distance. Wind whispers "freedom." The words give life to your broken heart. Wind continues to sing the song of freedom around you as it matches the pitch of the eagle. The song calms and then goes quiet. You open your eyes as Redeemer exclaims.

"You will be tempted by the hunger of success and accomplishment, and even times it will be posed as if you are doing it for me, but friend your motive must stay pure, and it must include me. You cannot live on success and satisfaction but only on every word that comes from the mouth of Love." Redeemer takes your hand in His and adds, "True success is sitting next to me, true accomplishment is embracing my goodness, doing my work is a lifestyle of love and repentance, as you continue to deny the idols and take my hand not defined by the world but known by me."

A wide smile spreads across your face as you lunge forward and wrap your arms around Redeemer's neck; He embraces you tightly back. The wind gently blows as a deep red fills the sky and the sun disappears behind the trees. Redeemer lets go and stands, then reaches His hand down which you grasp readily.

"Let's rest." The words are sweet as He lifts you to your feet and leads you back to the soft grass. You sit side by side resting your head against His shoulder. You close your eyes and fall into a deep slumber.

Chapter Five

Power of the Mind

Then the devil took him to the holy city and had him stand on the highest point of the temple. "If you are the Son of God," he said, "throw yourself down. For it is written: He will command his angels concerning you and they will lift you up in their hands, so that you will not strike your foot against a stone." Jesus answered him, "It is also written: Do not put the Lord your God to the test." - Matthew 4:5-7

The sun appears slowly creating a mist of dew throughout the trees. You awaken to birds chirping loudly. You lift your body from the cold hard ground and give a gentle stretch, lifting your arms to the sky. A slight yawn escapes from your lips as you rub your eyes. You bring your arms to your side and begin to look around for Redeemer: He is nowhere within sight. You stand to your feet and begin to pace around the grassy opening. As you closed your eyes last night, you remember distinctly resting against Him. He has been with you through the entirety of the journey and His company has been sweet and reassuring.

Panic begins to set in as you remember the solemn look on His face when He stared at the wood tablet filled with your accomplishments, and yet you missed the very essence of your life--being with Him. Redeemer is a new friend yet someone you have become so accustomed to having near you. His smile lights up your soul, and His very presence radiates Peace. Your pace turns frantic as you begin to venture away from the camp and into the morning fog.

"Redeemer!" the words quake from your lips as branches snap under your feet. With each step the dense fog engulfs you making it hard to see where you are going. You turn back around and see that the grassy opening is no longer in sight. *What have I done?* The thoughts make your heart race as you slowly move forward crying out "Redeemer!"

The somber forest grows even darker with each step; its density causes you to run into tree limbs and trip over logs. Defeated and completely blinded by the fog you rest against a tree unsure of where to turn next. The fog settles around you as a cool breeze whips against your skin. You wrap your arms tightly around your chest as a deep shiver runs up your spine. A loud slithering sound replaces the silence, and you begin to shudder. You look around frantically trying to locate where the sound is coming from. A small hiss catches your attention as you watch a snake slither down the tree across from you. The snake lifts half of its body off of the tree and out towards your face. Your eyes meet the eyes of the snake as he glides inches from your face.

Afraid, you quickly lunge your head back smashing it against the tree. You become dizzy as the snake stops moving and begins to slink in a crisscross pattern as his hazy blue eyes lock with yours. Your heart races with fear as you slowly move to the right bumping into another tree, his eyes continuing to pierce yours as you stare back intrigued.

"What's the matter friend?" the snake hisses as he continues to move back and forth.

Stunned by the talking snake you begin to stutter and shake. Tears fill your eyes as you press your body against the tree.

"Don't be afraid; I won't hurt you. I am here to help you find Redeemer."

"You know the Redeemer?" you reply between gulps with hesitation in your voice.

The leaves begin to rustle as a slight patter of rain falls from the clouds. Rain settles on the forest causing the fog to close in deeper forcing you to only see the snake.

"Of course, I do," the snake replies as he slithers closer to your face. "Why did Redeemer leave you? I thought he was your friend!"

"I.. I don't know. I awoke, and he was gone." Your hesitation begins to leave as you stare deep into the snake's eyes mesmerized by its blue depths.

The snake inches closer. "He is testing your patience to see if you will follow him into the forest."

The words roll off of the snake's tongue. Raindrops fall from the leaves and run down your face. You shiver and pull your arms tightly around your body.

"I love Redeemer and I would follow Him anywhere." The words fall fast from your tongue as you try to reassure the snake of your devotion.

"Is he as devoted to you as you are to him?"

The words of the snake cause confusion as he slithers within an inch of your face. His eyes begin to circle and you become dizzy and disoriented. You bring your hand to your head to stop the dizzy spell.

"Of course, He does; He would never let me down;" you say through your brain fog.

The snake begins to hiss the words, "Then why has he left you? If he is truly your friend, then command him to appear."

You quake under the words of the snake as darkness surrounds you, unable to cry out. The rain falls heavy as the snake lunges at your face sinking his fangs deep into your skull. You cry out in agony. Your body slams against the tree and then past it as you tumble backwards in a daze. You feel your body drop. You strike the ground with a thud and sink deep into a muddy hole. Pain races throughout your entire body as you flail about. You bring your knees to your chest and sit up as you sink deeper into the mud. Depression sets in as you sob into the wet soil and the rain pours heavily on top of you.

"Maybe He's not good; maybe He's not who He says He is; maybe He really isn't for me." The words pour out as you sob from your belly and rock back and forth trying to calm the racing pain in your body. Aches and pains shoot up your body as the mud engulfs you.

Eventually, your body grows weary from sobbing and the rain slows to a light drizzle. You feel the warmth of a small ray of sunlight form on the side of your face. You open your eyes and gaze upward as the sun shining bright overhead brings warmth to your tired face. You close your eyes as the sunlight fills the small line of vision created by its glow. Suddenly the sunlight turns to shade, and you open your eyes to see the outline of Redeemer staring down at you. You shudder from anger and turn from Him to stare back at the mud.

"What are you doing down there?" the words anger you so you yell back.

"You left me!" The words of anger turn to sadness as tears fall from your eyes.

Redeemer places His hand on the ledge of the hole in order to steady Himself as He leaps into the hole. He looks around at the mud and sits with His back against the edge as sunlight pours back into the hole.

You wipe the mud from your face, smearing it.

"I didn't leave you." The gentle words of Redeemer bring more tears to your eyes as you recognize the deep Love that shines in His eyes.

"When I awoke you were gone, so I stumbled into the forest to find you." The words come between sobs as your body shakes.

"Ahh friend," Redeemer inches in closer and places His hand on yours. "I wasn't gone, I was with my Father to prepare for today's activities. I wanted to let you rest as I communed with Love in the cool of the morning."

More tears fall from your eyes as you realize the deep mistake you have made. Redeemer reaches out and brushes the bite of the fang on your head tenderly with the tip of His finger. You wince as the pain rushes through your head. Redeemer smiles knowingly as He scoops up the tear-stained mud on His finger and places it tenderly on the bite. The pain suddenly eases and then leaves. You bring your fingers to the bite mark and can no longer feel it. Astonished, you gaze into Redeemer's eyes.

"The snake questioned your love for me, and I told him I would follow you anywhere, and then he made me lose doubt in you and I believed him. I tried to cry out for you, but words would not come, and I found myself in deep despair questioning everything."

The tears begin to fall once again. Redeemer moves in closer.

"Friend, he too tempted me by challenging me to test my Father, Love. The scripture which says to never test God. Much like you must never test the power of my redemption. Just because you didn't see me does not mean I was not there."

"I don't understand what you mean."

Redeemer smiles as He takes your hand. "Friend, the tempter questioned your devotion to me, and you instantly wanted to prove your devotion. He then questioned my devotion to you planting seeds of doubt, and still you felt to prove your devotion. Devotion is a decision of the heart; it will never need to be proved. Devotion reflects being close to me. If you leave the camp without me, you will open yourself up to the tempter, and you will face him alone. He is sly and plants thoughts of doubt concerning my nature. However, if you leave the camp with me and the tempter comes, you will not be shaken with doubt, because I will be standing next to you sharing the truth."

The words of Redeemer bring clarity as you inch closer to Him. The sun brightens the entirety of the hole as the birds begin to chirp. Redeemer wraps His arms around you and brings you close to His chest.

"What about the bite mark, why did he bite me?"

Redeemer brings His finger to your forehead and points. "The power of your thoughts. You accepted the lie and doubted what you know is true concerning me; therefore, it gave the tempter the leverage he needed to strike. You spiraled into a hole of pain and depression, but friend, I will always come to your rescue; it's my nature. You must remember that the tempter will try to place doubt in your mind concerning your identity in me and, if that doesn't work, then he will try to place doubt in your mind concerning my nature. He tempted me, and he will tempt you. But resist the lies, cling to the truth, and stay close to me."

Redeemer unwraps His arms from you and wipes the mud from your tear-streaked face. He stands to His feet and pulls you out of the mud. "Come on friend, I have someone I want you to meet."

The insistent words of Redeemer bring excitement to your soul as the fear and depression vanish and joy is restored. Redeemer places His hand on the top of the ledge of the hole and pulls Himself out. He extends His hand down, and you grasp it as he lifts you from your hole. Once on solid ground you take in the view as a clearing appears amongst the trees.

Redeemer turns and smiles. "Race you!"

He takes off like a giddy kid and your heart races with excitement as your legs carry you through the forest and into the clearing as you follow after Redeemer.

Chapter Six

Shield of Faith

Again, the devil took him to a very high mountain and showed him all the kingdoms of the world and their splendor. "All this I will give you," he said, "if you will bow down and worship me." Jesus said to him, "Away from me, Satan! For it is written: Worship the Lord your God, and serve him only." Then the devil left him, and angels came and attended him. - Matthew 4:5-7

You come to an abrupt stop as you run into the clearing. With the forest behind you, you search for Redeemer. Your gaze takes in the blue sky as you see a city off in the distance. The birds chirp loudly and a cool breeze tickles your face. You scan the horizon and look down at your shoes caked with dry mud, and your clothing is heavy with it. Without hesitation you begin to run towards the hustle and bustle of the busy city.

The journey is easy as you gain distance between you and the forest behind you. Your run turns to a light jog as you find a song in your heart and begin to whistle. A gentle breeze brings great relief from the sun. You reach the edge of the city. You turn and look as people rush by on foot. The old buildings display great architecture and years of history. You walk past the city walls and find yourself in the middle of a market filled with people.

Shield of Faith

Off to your right you see an old beggar, dirty and hungry. On your left you see a man well-dressed and trading money for goods. People don't seem to notice you as you stroll through running your hands along beautiful items. You are impressed first with a table filled with fabrics and lovely glass vases. You stop and ponder the items as you trace your finger along each design. People move throughout the market pushing and fighting their way through others to purchase what they want.

The chatter in the market grows loud as a woman trips over the old beggar. You turn towards the scene as the woman yells, "Move!" The old beggar keeps her head down and scoots back into the shadows. You look back at the fabric and once again run your hand across the perfect, neatly sewn bead work. You move to the next table display just a few feet away and find a bounty of crops: corn and beans ripe and ready for purchase. As you reach down to pick up some corn, a stranger rams into you. Stunned, you back away as people run into each other fighting to get in line and make their purchases. Once again you turn around as another stir breaks out in the corner when a man runs into the old beggar yelling, "Get out of here, you are not wanted." The old beggar once again scoots back into the shadows with her head down.

You move past the crops and to a stand filled with perfect gold coins. You pick up the coins and run them through your fingers tracing each one with your finger. Your desire for one of these coins grows as you examine the table filled with them and search for the perfect one. A man bumps into you, and you find your footing as you step back to catch yourself. Frustrated, you step forward and shove him back with your shoulder fighting for a spot at the table. You place your finger on another coin as a woman pushes through the crowd elbowing your side. You step back and trip over someone's foot as your body lands on the ground. You gaze up to see the table now surrounded by people pressing against it with no way for you to get back in. You wipe your brow and hurry away from the huddle of stomping feet and loud chatter. You turn your gaze and find the old beggar staring at you. The old woman's eyes are filled with fire and kindness as they gaze into yours.

People begin to trip over you as they shove towards the table filled with coins. You wince as you get kicked and unkind words are spat at you. You begin to crawl to the woman in the corner. Once safe in the shadows, you turn and watch as the hustle continues. Your eyes turn back and meet the eyes of the woman. You give a weak smile.

"The least of these will be the greatest in the Kingdom of God."

Startled by her words, you lean in. "Kingdom of God? Aren't you hungry and miserable?"

The old woman reaches out her hand and pats yours. "I am not from this Kingdom. Also," she whispers and leans in close, "my friend Redeemer takes care of all of my needs."

You scan her clothing which is dirty and ragged. Her frail bones and thin stature are evidence of hunger. *Well, He is not doing a very good job*, you think to yourself.

The woman stares deep into your eyes without saying a word. She scans your dry muddy clothing and filthy hands. You shudder under the intensity. Out of the corner of your eye a light pierces the distance. You turn your head and see Redeemer on the outskirts of the city scanning the crowd.

"Go to Him."

The old woman's words startle you, as you turn and give her a weak smile and jump to your feet. You run past the people in the market, shoving your way through the crowd. You continue to run out of the market past the buildings and into the outskirts of the city. You reach Redeemer and throw your arms around Him.

He embraces you tightly saying, "Where have you been?"

You loosen yourself from His arms and stare into His eyes. "I was in the most beautiful market filled with fabrics, glass vases, crops, and the most intriguing gold coins."

You turn back to face the market longing to see the items once again.

"Ahh," Redeemer says as He turns on His heels and begins walking away from the city. You follow instinctively.

"I also met a woman who said she was your friend. She was an old beggar though and unwell; surely she is not someone you know?"

Redeemer continues to walk, as a cool breeze races past Him. Redeemer looks to the path that you walked down just hours ago and begins to walk towards the forest.

"And why would I not know her?" He asks cautiously as you trail behind him.

Chosen

"Well, she is dirty and hungry. She says you take care of her, but you are good and kind. You would not let one of your friends suffer like that."

"Indeed, but not everything is as perceived." Redeemer continues walking.

You follow closely waiting for an answer, and your weary body slows its pace. The hot sun beats down on you as you stare off in the distance slowly taking each step. Redeemer remains silent reaching the clearing on the outskirts of the forest. You watch as the sun seems to stand still, your entire body shaking from exhaustion. You turn slightly and see Redeemer sitting in the shade under a tree trying to catch His breath. You walk a few steps until the shade engulfs you and sit next to Him and gaze down trying and catch your breath.

"Look!" The excitement in Redeemer's voice causes you to gaze up.

Standing before you is the most exquisite woman you have ever seen. Her long auburn hair blows in the wind as her small frame stands before you. You gaze up into her hazel eyes and gasp at the fire you see in them. You recognize her eyes as those of the old beggar. You turn to Redeemer.

He smiles and says, "This is my friend, Lesson."

You turn back from Redeemer and find Lesson standing tall. She reaches for her shoulders and removes something from her back, then kneels down and hands you the most beautiful shield you have ever seen.

Shield of Faith

"The shield of faith," she says as she moves with grace to extend the shield as she bows her head. You turn and look at Redeemer questioningly and He nods. You place your hands on the shield and pull it to your chest.

Lesson smiles. "The shield of faith stops the fiery darts of the enemy. The enemy uses judgement to derail us. You may perceive one's journey based upon their outside appearance, but you have no idea the journey that is happening within. This is where faith comes in--faith in Redeemer. That only He knows what journey each person is on. You, friend, were so consumed with your own material wants that you did not approach me until you were on the same level as me, and even then, you were repulsed by my outer countenance; but what you didn't see was what Redeemer was doing in my heart."

Tears form in your eyes as you now see who Lesson truly is: a daughter loved and chosen. You turn to Redeemer, and He smiles.

"How could I have been so blind?" you gasp.

"Not blind but consumed by what this world has to offer. It offers nothing good compared to what Redeemer can give you." Lesson continues, "True goodness comes from our inner treasure and gain, the places that no one else can see. The things of this world truly will pass away, like fog in the morning, but the will of Redeemer remains. Pick up your shield of faith, friend, trust the process, quench the fiery darts of judgement, do not let it overtake you."

Lesson leans in and grasps your hand pulling your shield out in front of you. "Do not fall prey to thinking that the things of this world are Redeemer's blessings. True blessing comes from within. He cares for His friends and wants good things for them but, above all else, He wants them to have healthy hearts. Use your shield of faith to protect your heart. Do not fall prey to worshiping the things of this world. Worship only the one true God." Lesson stands and smiles at Redeemer, then she turns and walks away. You turn to Redeemer.

"The last temptation, friend. I, too, was tempted with the keys of this Kingdom's splendor, but nothing compares to the splendor of the Kingdom of God. I did eventually obtain the keys of this Kingdom though but not by bowing down to a false god. There is only one true God, but that's a story for another day" Redeemer gives a slight wink as a smile spreads across your face. "Keep your eyes on me and Love, the one true God. That should be where your utmost honor is displayed."

Chapter Seven

One More Step

The Lord is not slow to fulfill his promise as some count slowness, but is patient toward you, not wishing that any should perish, but that all should reach repentance. - 2 Peter 3:9

Still holding your shield, you watch as Redeemer stands and follows Lesson. His white cloak fades into the distance as He rounds a bend. The pink sky turns to a dark purple as the stars begin to fill the sky. You stand up, still intrigued by Lesson's words. You slip your arms through the straps on the back of the shield and place it on your back.

The night air shoots a chill up your spine. You cross your arms tightly across your chest, then you turn and walk towards the bend and make a turn around the corner looking for Redeemer. You walk to the edge of the cliff and look down to find a staircase. *Surely Redeemer went down the staircase,* you think out loud and take a cautious first step onto the stairs. "Redeemer!" Your voice cracks as you call out the word. The air is calm and all of creation is still. The sky has turned black, and the only light left is that of the large round moon radiating only enough light to see the stair step in front of you. You move your left leg carefully and feel the firm step of rock beneath you. You scan the rocks around you and the darkness shoots fear throughout your entire body.

Chosen

The chill of the wind nips your ears and nose as night sets in. You gaze down at the next step and squint your eyes to try and make out its shape. You begin to tremble as you slowly place a shaky leg down onto the next step. "How long will this go on?" you whisper as you bring your other leg onto the firm rock below. The sound of falling rocks startles you as you whip your head up and gaze to your right. You can see the outline of a few rock formations within the darkness and nothing more. You move your hand to feel for a rock wall next to the stairs, but your hand flies through open air. You become distinctly aware that one wrong step to the right and you will fall off the stairs and straight to the bottom of the canyon.

Your legs begin to tremble as fear settles deep within your belly. You sit quickly on the dark stairs bracing your body upright with your hands, afraid your shaky legs will cause you to stumble. The moon casts a shadow down the eerie canyon stairs. You hear an owl begin to hoot, and the sound startles you as you slowly stand. A sense of urgency prompts you to keep moving. A familiar breeze of Wind blows across your face, and you gasp with joy as a familiar friend nestles behind your neck. "Endure my friend, you must keep going, not quickly though, move slowly" As quickly as the words left, so did Wind. You gasp exasperated as you take another shaky step down but this time very slowly.

You feel the sturdiness of the rocky step below, then you bring your other foot down on the rock. Your eyes begin to adjust to the darkness as you scan the canyon. You gaze behind, impressed with how far you have come. You estimate that you are about halfway down the stairs. A gentle hum begins to form as you graciously clear another step. Your legs begin to settle under you and your racing heart slows. You take in the stars and notice they fill the entire sky without an end in sight. You breathe in the night air as you continue down the narrowing steps.

Step after step, your weary legs glide you down the dark canyon. Your ears perk up when you hear a faint sound of rushing water in the distance. It sounds as though it is hitting the bottom of the canyon. You begin to quicken your pace as you clear another round of stairs. The water grows louder under the starry sky. The excitement causes you to move too quickly onto a narrowing step, your foot slips, and you find yourself sliding down the stairs, hitting your rear with a thud. You reach out to stop yourself from sliding and your hand only catches air. Your body jolts to a halt, and you realize the stairs have become so narrow that you can only use one hand to steady your body. Your heart begins to race and panic sets in. The moon illuminates the staircase as you look over the edge into the canyon floor. *Slow and steady* you remind yourself as you push yourself back onto your feet, determined to get to the sound of the rushing water.

Your body aches with pain as you find your footing on the next rock, taking one cautious step after the other for what seems like an eternity. The sound of the water grows louder as the sky begins to form the lighter hues of morning. With your hands extended to steady your balance, you look down to see that the narrowing staircase now only fits your feet without any room to sit. After a deep breath, you gaze into the rising sun. As you cautiously clear another step, the sound of water grows louder. Suddenly you are gazing at the most breathtaking waterfall that you have ever seen. The waterfall begins at the top of the canyon and flows gently down the rocks into a crystal-clear pool below. The sun clears the top of the canyon with a pink hue. On every side of the waterfall is a canyon.

You gaze down and see you only have a few steps left. You leap down each one gracefully and begin to run towards the magnificent waterfall. The wind blows against your face as you race to reach the crystal-clear pool. Your run slows to a walk as you begin to climb the rocks surrounding the pool. The waterfall roars and water falls heavily into the pool forming at the bottom. As you pull yourself onto the rock, you peer into the crystal-clear water and are met with your own reflection. You see dirt stains covering your cheeks; your eyes are weary and unrecognizable. You wipe your messy hair from your forehead as the exhausted image of you stares back. You gaze back down at your dirty clothing and sigh.

The sound of laughter startles you as you look up. Your eyes see a beautiful woman with waist-length black hair dancing under the waterfall. Her laugh penetrates your ears as she spins with delight. Her white flowy dress dances across the rock as she skips, tucked safely behind the rushing falls. You watch as she innocently runs her hand through the waterfall, parting the water with her fingers. Her hazel eyes gaze up and lock with your own. A perfect smile spreads across her face as she waves in your direction. You gingerly wave back with an exhausted energy. She turns from the water and walks behind a rock out of sight. You scan the rocks trying to find a way to get to her. The sun grows heavy in the sky.

You wipe the sweat from your brow, and with a defeated sigh, you jump into the crystal- clear water. As you come up for air, you begin to swim frantically towards the waterfall. You leave a wake of dirty water from your journey. You swim harder, and yet the murky water lurks around you. You find your footing at the base of the waterfall. The sound of the crashing falls are loud in your ears as you wade through the water. You duck your head as your body breaks the waterfall causing you to stumble and fall. You catch yourself with your hands and begin to crawl towards the rock as the water falls hard against your body causing you to fall on your face. You manage to get out from the break of the water and lay flat on your belly as your heavy breathing begins to slow.

You pick up your head and wipe the water from your eyes. You turn your body to a sitting position and look down at the cuts and scratches fresh from the rocks. You bring your gaze to the filthy, murky water as the waterfall crashes below. Exhausted, drenched, and in pain, you push yourself to your feet and take a shaky step towards the rock. As you reach the rock and peer behind, you find the woman sitting outstretched with her eyes closed and her face turned upward towards the sun. Her skin is perfect, and her long hair lain gently at her side. You sit quietly a few feet away as you draw your scraped legs closely to your chest.

The woman opens her eyes and gazes at you with a smile. "Hello friend." Her voice sounds like the water and a smile forms from the corner of your mouth. The woman stands to her feet and reaches within her pocket pulling out a jar of paste. She steps towards you and gently gives you the jar. You take the jar with questioning eyes. She smiles. "For your legs." You reach your finger inside to scoop up the paste and administer it lightly to your wounds. To your amazement the wounds begin to heal under the fragrance of the paste. The woman once again sits and closes her eyes as the sun dances on her face.

"Who are you?" you ask quietly as you continue to put the paste on your remaining wounds.

"A Friend," the words roll off her tongue as she remains in the same position.

You put the paste down next to you as you gaze at your clear legs, waiting for the woman to say more. She stands quietly and brushes past you. She looks behind her shoulder at you.

"Come, friend, it's time to dance in the waterfall."

You jump to your feet and follow her past the rock and back under the crashing falls. Your eyes catch the face of Redeemer, the woman runs towards Him; He catches her hand and gives her a gentle spin. Both Redeemer and the woman begin to laugh. You watch them dance together, happy, and carefree.

"Friend, I have missed you." The voice of Redeemer meshes with the sound of the waterfall as you begin to walk towards Him.

He matches your step and meets you in the middle. With His arms stretched wide you fall into them as He wraps you in a strong embrace.

"You did it!" The words ring in your ears as He gazes into your eyes.

You see the woman out of the corner of your eye as she begins to spin under the waterfall. Redeemer laughs as He takes your hand and begins to spin you, the water splashes on your face. You let go of Redeemer's hand and begin to jump and laugh as water splashes around you. The strong water rushes as you weave in and out of the water. The woman and Redeemer spin and run next to you. A deep laugh radiates out of you as you allow playfulness to enter your heart. The laugh causes you to sit back behind the waterfall, Redeemer sits next to you. You rest your head on His shoulder and gaze out at the crystal-clear pool.

"There is nothing too dirty for me to make clean." The words from Redeemer calm your spirit as you gaze into His eyes.

The woman sits next to you and wraps her arm around your arm. She gently strokes your hair.

"One slow step at a time is how we make it to the most beautiful places," she says.

You turn and your eyes meet with a smile. You nod knowingly and turn your gaze back to the water. You feel Redeemer and the woman stand and walk behind you, as you remain lost in your reveries.

Chapter Eight

In the Boat

Jesus said to him, "I am the way, and the truth, and the life. No one comes to the Father except through me." - John 14:6

The breeze dances across your face as the cool of the day sets deep within the canyon. Your eyes continue to gaze into the crystal lake, until you become restless. You stand and scan the rocks behind you. You adjust your shield gently on your back and adjust your breastplate back in place.

Your eyes trace the side of the tall canyon as the evening sun reflects a warm glow off of the side. You walk back under the waterfall as the cool water lightly splashes against your arm. "One slow step is how I find beautiful things," you repeat the words of the woman as you continue to walk under the waterfall. You let your pace drop to a slow walk as you reach out your hand and allow your fingers to touch the falling water. The warmth of the sun finds your face as you close your eyes and let it soothe your soul. You are jolted to your senses as a crash and thud draw your eyes past the waterfall and to the edge of the crystal lake. To your delight you catch the fiery eyes and warm smile of Redeemer. He is ankle-deep in water as he motions you to come to Him. You walk cautiously making sure not to slip from the pressure of the falls.

In the Boat

Once through the waterfall, you trudge through the crystal lake knee-deep in water.

Redeemer's eyes shine brightly as He watches you cross through the lake towards Him. He steadies a small, wooden boat. As you approach Redeemer, you see mischief in His eyes.

"Come on," Redeemer says with excitement in His voice. "Get in" His words are followed by laughter. A wide smile spreads across your face and you shake your head knowing this is going to be a fun adventure. You grab the edge of the boat and leap in as Redeemer steadies it beneath you before jumping in Himself. He pushes the boat from the shore of the canyon with ease.

Sitting across from Redeemer, you watch as He rows the boat through the crystal lake. His eyes meet yours and, with a crooked smile, He gives you a wink. You turn your attention from Redeemer and gaze ahead as the boat glides along. The sound of the waterfall grows quieter as you row between the canyon and down a gentle stream.

"Where are we going?" your voice quakes with excitement.

"Ahh, we are going fishing," He replies, and deep down you have a feeling it isn't going to be a normal fishing trip.

The sun bounces off the lake casting an orange glow over the tips of the canyon. You gaze into the stream below and are overcome with the clarity in your eyes. You look up to find a beautiful clearing. Redeemer rows intently as the clearing becomes more visible. No longer in the split of the canyon, Redeemer stops rowing and allows the boat to remain still in the middle of the clearing. A cool breeze dances over the water. Redeemer reaches down to the floor of the boat and pulls out two fishing poles. He hands one to you and flicks a gentle perfect cast to the right of the boat.

"Wow, that was a perfect cast!" you exclaim as you grasp your pole.

Redeemer slowly begins reeling in the cast as He turns His head towards you. "I have had a lot of practice," He laughs gently.

You turn your attention to your own pole and let out a flick of the wrist as your line goes sailing through the air and plops right in front of the boat. Embarrassed and ashamed of your cast, you reel it in as fast as you can and give another aggressive flick of the wrist. The line goes sailing once again as it wraps itself around the pole and plops in front of the boat.

"This pole is broken," you say and turn to Redeemer as frustration sets in.

"It's not broken; you are missing the key to fishing: patience." Redeemer speaks slowly as His eyes stay focused on His pole, and with the flick of a wrist the cast falls perfectly into the water. Heat burns your cheeks as embarrassment sets in once again. You untwist the line from your pole and gently reel it in. With a deep breath, you let out a gentle flick of your wrist and watch your line soar and plop a good distance away.

"You don't need to prove yourself to me. I am already proud of you." His words bring tears to your eyes as you reel the line in slowly.

In the Boat

Redeemer lets out another perfect cast as the sun disappears behind the clouds. You watch your line intently as you reel it in and give another gentle cast.

"Being a fisher of men takes patience and endurance, but it mostly takes knowledge that you don't have to prove yourself to anyone, especially me."

You sit your pole down next to you and gaze upon Redeemer, He releases another perfect cast and studies the line as He slowly reels it in.

"But I get so easily discouraged, and sometimes it feels like I have to prove myself to you, to prove that I am worth loving, I am worth protecting, I am worth seeing. What's the secret to overcoming these feelings?" The words end in a choke as you hold back tears.

Redeemer releases another cast, and you watch as it gracefully hits the water. The sun casts a purple hue over the water. You stare out over the water with a worried expression.

"Friend, don't put down your pole, even when you don't feel me--don't put down your pole."

This advice startles you. You turn from the water and, frustrated, quickly grab your pole and cast it into the water. You feel that Redeemer has not fully answered your questions. You watch as your line soars in the air then tangles and plops in the water. Your frustration turns to anger, you drop your pole in the boat and cover your face. Redeemer sets His pole gently at His side and reaches for yours before slowly untangling the mess of the line. He reaches His hand out motioning for you to take the pole.

You uncover your face and look at Him with probing eyes. He nods gently, and you take the pole back in your hand.

He wraps His hand around yours and together you release the perfect cast. You watch as the line soars through the air and lands perfectly in the water. Excitement rushes through your heart as you turn and look at Redeemer. He smiles, then leans in closely: "The secret is abiding in me."

You study Redeemer's face. He smiles and sits back, then He releases another perfect cast.

"You are worth loving; you are worth protecting; you are seen. You will only know this truth by abiding in me."

His eyes glisten, and the words penetrate your heart. You feel a tug on your line and, with excitement, you reel in slowly but firmly against the line's resistance. The pole turns to the right and left, you give a strong tug. You continue to reel and tug until you pull the perfect fish out of the water.

Redeemer gazes at the fish.

"Ahh, perfect catch friend."

Your heart skips a beat as you unhook the fish and place it back in the water and lay the pole by your side. The evening sky turns to a dark blue as little stars begin to appear. You turn and look into the eyes of Redeemer. Redeemer strokes your cheek.

"You are a fisher of men. The catch takes patience, resilience, and abiding. This fish is one of many. You, my friend, have been faithful." The words of Redeemer bring an instant calm to your body.

In the Boat

The stars shine bright in the sky, while the moon casts a perfect glow from its reflection in the lake. You lean back and rest against your seat in the boat. Your eyelids become heavy, and you close your eyes. Redeemer begins to hum; He then sings the words "Abiding is only done through fixating your gaze on me. Endure, endure, endure oh sojourner, then you will abide in the house of the Lord." A deep slumber comes over you as you hear the words to the song. An array of colors dance in your mind as your body slumps down onto the floor of the boat. The slumber is deep, and your entire body succumbs to a strong sense of peace that settles in your bones.

Chapter Nine

Helmet of Salvation

Put on salvation as your helmet, and take the sword of the Spirit, which is the word of God. - Ephesians 6:17

The sun casts bright lights behind your closed eyes. Warmth spreads across your face as you awaken to the noon day sun shining brightly on your face. You place your hands at your side and feel a hard rock beneath your fingers. You sit up and find yourself sitting once again behind the waterfall, no longer in the boat. The roar of the waterfall is now a familiar sound. You see Redeemer walking through the shallow of the water. You stand and brush off some dirt. You clean your shoes and your breastplate, then you reach behind and pull the shield off your back. You remove dirt from your shield and place it back behind you, fitting the straps tightly on your shoulders.

You feel a deep sense of peace as you stride towards Redeemer. He smiles and His eyes shine with goodness.

"Good morning, friend." The kindness in His voice makes your heart leap.

"Good morning. How did I get here?"

Helmet of Salvation

"Ahh, you fell into a deep healing slumber within my presence, and I carried you from the boat to the shore so you could rest peacefully."

"Healing presence? What is that?"

Redeemer's eyes twinkle as He responds, "Let me show you."

With a wave of His hand, He guides you back behind the waterfall and between the rocks.

You walk closely behind Redeemer and are amazed by the colors reflecting off the rock structure. The sun warms your skin; the roar of the waterfall becomes distant. As you walk further between the rocks, you make out a clearing in the distance. The pleasant chirping of birds grows louder. You watch as Redeemer strides through the rocks into the clearing. You follow closely and, to your amazement, you are met with the most beautiful sight in the center of the canyon. Lush green grass stands tall all around. The sky is a piercing blue as the sun lights up the canyon. Birds fly overhead and deer run gently with their fawns.

Giant rocks surround all sides of the canyon. A great feeling of security fills you. You spin around joyfully as deep laughter roars from your belly. You turn and find Redeemer mimicking you. You laugh harder and join your hands with Him and spin together. Redeemer's laugh sounds like water. You sink to your knees and he meets you on the ground.

With a gentle gaze He proclaims, "Let's go!"

He grabs your hand and lifts you up and, with a wink, He races quickly before you. You race after Him through one end of the canyon to the next. Once you reach the other end of the canyon, Redeemer's pace slows as He walks quietly through a narrow passageway. You follow closely and see Redeemer lean down and pick up a small pickaxe lying next to a rock wall. He extends the pickaxe and you take it cautiously.

"It's time to chisel the rock away."

Redeemer points to a spot in the rock wall. Confused, you place both hands on the pickaxe and, with a large swing, it strikes the side of the narrow canyon. A small chip of rock breaks off, and with another great swing the pickaxe strikes the rock again. Two, three, four more swings as rock breaks off the side of the rock wall. Sweat begins to form across your brow and you turn to Redeemer. A smile spreads across His face, and He encourages you to continue to strike the rock. One, two, three, four more swings and shooting pain rushes up your arm. You lay the pickaxe on the ground for a moment as you wipe your brow. You gaze at the small dent you have made in the side of the rock wall and become discouraged. You turn around again and gaze at Redeemer who nods again. You pick up the pickaxe and strike the rock again, over and over and over, until your body sinks to the floor of the canyon.

"I can't go on. I am not even making a dent."

Redeemer kneels next to you, reaches down, picks up the pickaxe, then begins to strike the rock with brute force. Still kneeling, you watch as rocks fall while Redeemer wields the pickaxe and strikes repeatedly. He stops and wipes His brow. You scoot a few feet away so rock will not fall on you. Redeemer brings the pickaxe behind His

Helmet of Salvation

shoulder—one, two, three, four more swings. Large rocks fall again. Redeemer swings the pickaxe and strikes again, over, and over and over, until a perfect hole forms inside of the rock wall.

Redeemer puts the pickaxe down and walks towards you. He extends His hand, and you grasp on. Redeemer pulls you to your feet.

"Go and see," He says.

With a weary sigh, you walk over the fallen rocks. You gaze into the perfect hole formed in the side of the rock canyon. Your eyes widen with amazement as you see a beautiful gold helmet shining brightly. You turn to Redeemer.

He smiles and nods. "Go ahead, grab it."

You reach into the hole and carefully remove the helmet. You hold it out in front of you. You regard Redeemer with a quizzical look.

"What is it?"

"The helmet of salvation," Redeemer exclaims excitedly.

You walk closer to Redeemer and extend it towards Him. "What is it for?"

Redeemer runs His hand across the top of the helmet and gazes into your eyes.

"It's a physical representation of the deliverance from harm, ruin, loss, and sin. The ultimate price that was paid for you. The helmet protects your mind from the confusion and schemes of the enemy. The helmet also supports the crest. The helmet represents your rank in my army as a friend and child. Your salvation grants you the position to walk in the love, power, and authority granted to you through my sacrifice."

Tears sting your eyes as recognition of this power surges through your body.

"Never forget," Redeemer continues with a stern look in His eyes, "this is not something you can earn through your own strength. Just like you were unable to create the hole in the side of the rock, you are unable to earn or create salvation. It is simply a gift that requires a sacrifice on my part but is freely given to you, you must simply accept it."

Redeemer grabs the helmet from your hand and places it on your head. He lifts the face shield and looks lovingly into your eyes.

"I only ask that you do not remove it, and that you allow me to be your guide. The gift cannot be obtained on its own; it comes in relationship with me. Position and authority come with guidance and wisdom. I am your guide and your source of all wisdom."

You nod knowingly. Redeemer grabs your hand and guides you back to the lush grass in the canyon. You cling to His hand tightly and follow His steps. The air is cool as a gentle breeze blows. You stop and look up at Redeemer. He brings His hand to your face shield and flips it down.

"When your face shield covers your eyes, the enemy can't tell if he is fighting you or me." Redeemer gives you a wink and, with a pat against your breastplate, proclaims, "It's time to go!"

Helmet of Salvation

The grass beneath your feet is soft as you glance down at your shoes of the gospel of peace, place your hand on your breastplate of righteousness, and once again feel your heart beating. You straighten your shoulder straps that hold your shield of faith in place. You turn your head from side to side to adjust to the heavy helmet of salvation. You make certain that it fits snugly and follow Redeemer out of the lush canyon. You pick up your pace trying to catch up to Him as He walks swiftly through the canyon and back through the rocks. You find yourself once again in the water a few steps away from the boat.

You pause as your eyes take in the grandness and cool water splashes against your arms and legs. You catch Redeemer's hand motioning you to hurry as He gets in the rickety boat. You trudge through the knee-deep water, flinging your body over the side of the boat and sitting across from Redeemer as He begins to row.

Chapter Ten

Kindness of Redeemer

And he gave some, apostles; and some, prophets; and some, evangelists; and some, pastors and teachers; For the perfecting of the saints, for the work of the ministry, for the edifying of the body of Christ. - Ephesians 4:11-12

"Where are we going?"

Redeemer furrows His brow and, with a stern look, responds, "I must make you aware of something happening right now."

You glance down in the water. You bring your hand to your face shield and flip it up as you stare deeply into your own reflection. The boat clears the side of the canyon and comes into a clearing as Redeemer rows it to a nearby shore. He places the paddles in the bottom of the boat and jumps out. You flip your face shield down and jump out behind Him. Walking quickly once again to match His pace, you follow Redeemer trudging through a valley and up a grassy hill.

You follow closely as you attempt to catch your breath as you reach the top of the hill. Redeemer stands staring into a valley below. Your gaze catches five tribes working diligently on specific assignments. You turn to speak to Redeemer, but He brings His finger to His lips motioning you to stay quiet as He sits down. He pats a grassy spot next to Him and you join Him. You watch each tribe intently. The first tribe frantically writes details on a scroll. The second tribe unrolls a map and points to multiple places. The third tribe makes footsteps in the sand gaining ground. The fourth tribe gathers and tends to the members of their tribe. The fifth and final tribe gives clear and concise instructions to the members of their tribe.

You turn your eyes from the valley and stare up at Redeemer. His face is stoic yet calm. A cool breeze rushes through the air carrying the sounds of bickering and division. You also hear the tones of secrecy and hushed plans. You bring your eyes back to the valley as tribes look over their shoulders and spew angry words at one another. The fighting and bickering grow louder carried within the wind. You grow unsettled and frustrated by the continuum of work, as each specific assignment from each tribe repeats a cycle that seems to never advance.

"My friends," Redeemer says, still gazing into the valley, "their love for me is pure and they take their assignment very seriously, but they are unable to work together." Redeemer stands and adds, "Come, it's time to meet my friends."

You stand quickly, your legs begin to tremble, and you slowly follow Redeemer down the hill into the valley. Redeemer approaches the first tribe.

"These are my apostles. They carry great wisdom to write out the plans for the next assignment."

The tribe senses Redeemer's presence and they fall to the ground in His presence. The leader of the tribe stands and speaks.

Chosen

"Our King, oh Mighty one, can you sense it? We are using the wisdom you have given us in great detail."

The leader bows his head then looks up to Redeemer who places His hand on the leader's shoulder.

"You have written great details, but you must learn to work with the other tribes."

The leader stares blankly at Redeemer, then he turns and motions for his tribe to get back to work. Redeemer turns to you.

"My apostles' write great details but without the others their details will do nothing to advance them."

Redeemer turns from their camp and enters the camp of the second tribe. "These are my prophets. They carry great vision to see and uncover routes that will lead them to their next assignment."

The tribe notices Redeemer's presence and they fall to the ground in His presence. Then the leader of the tribe stands.

"Our Majesty, oh Glorious one, have you noticed? We are using the vision you have given us to uncover the best route to take." The leader bows his head then looks up to Redeemer who takes the leader's hand.

"You have uncovered the route clearly, but you must learn to work with the other tribes."

The leader stares blankly at Redeemer. He turns and motions for His tribe to get back to work uncovering the route. Redeemer turns to you.

Kindness of Redeemer

"My prophets carry great vision to see the land clearly but, without the others, their vision will carry no substance."

Redeemer walks through their camp and enters the camp of the third tribe.

"These are my evangelists. They carry great zeal into the new territory with fire and passion propelling them to their next assignment."

The tribe feels Redeemer's presence and they fall to the ground in His presence. The leader of the tribe stands.

"Our Lord, oh Magnificent one, can you feel it? We are using the zeal you have given us to make clear footsteps."

The leader bows his head. Redeemer lifts the leader's chin up.

"You have gained ground correctly, but you must learn to work with others."

The leader stares blankly at Redeemer. He turns and motions for his tribe to get back to work creating footsteps. Redeemer turns to you.

"My Evangelists carry great zeal but, without wisdom and direction from the others, they will fail."

Redeemer removes himself from their camp and into the camp of the fourth tribe.

"These are my pastors. They carry great compassion and stewardship as they prepare their tribe for their next assignment."

Chosen

The tribe sees Redeemer and they fall to the ground in His presence. The leader of the tribe stands.

"Our Ruler, oh Sovereign One, have you seen? We are using the compassion you have given us to clearly prepare our tribe."

The leader bows and lifts his head. Redeemer gazes into the leader's eyes.

"You have prepared your tribe correctly, but you must learn to work with the others."

The leader stares blankly at Redeemer. He turns and motions for his tribe to get back to work compassionately preparing others. Redeemer turns to you.

"My pastors shepherd with great compassion but, without balance and help, they will become exhausted and quit."

Redeemer walks around their camp and into the camp of the fifth and final tribe.

"These are my teachers. They carry great ambition as they give concise teaching to their tribe for their next assignment."

The tribe hears Redeemer's footsteps while teaching their members, and they fall to the ground in His presence. The leader of the tribe stands.

"Our Provider, oh Merciful One, can you hear it? We are using the ambition you have given us to clearly teach our tribe with clear instructions."

The leader bows and lifts his head. Redeemer strokes the leader's cheek.

"You have taught your tribe correctly, but you must learn to work with the others."

The leader stares blankly at Redeemer, then he turns and motions for his tribe to get back to work teaching others. Redeemer turns to you.

"My teachers instruct with strong ambition but, without the leadership of others, their teaching will be swayed."

Redeemer shakes His head and walks slowly past the camp and begins back up the hill. You follow closely as the sun sets within the cool breeze of the sky. Redeemer stops on the top of the hill.

"How long must I be with them? Heed my instruction: the tribes must use their gifting in unison, only then will they experience my fullness."

Redeemer begins walking down the other side of the hill.

You hear him say, "I am with them always, but there is coming a time when great deception will cause great division. They must learn to work together, step by step. That will be their strongest chance against the division."

You follow Redeemer closely as you walk through the valley surrounded by tall grass and flowers. Your eyes catch an old man in the distance and watch as Redeemer picks up His pace and excitedly runs to Him. You follow in their direction. You reach Redeemer and He smiles.

"This is my friend, Kin."

Your eyes make out a round old face with wrinkles formed in the creases of his eyes as a giant smile spreads across his face. His eyes are a deep green that changes slightly in the sunlight. His old, gentle stature infused with wisdom takes a step towards you. Your eyes glance down to his wrinkled hand holding a pure white flower placed securely between his fingers. You glance back at Redeemer. He nods and smiles again.

"I am going to give you two a moment alone."

You watch Redeemer walk away. You long to follow Him but bring your eyes back to the old man and smile back at him weakly.

"How about a walk?"

The words sound gruff as Kin begins walking. You follow quietly looking down at your feet. The grass covers your ankles, the wind is cool, and the sun hides behind the clouds. Kin turns abruptly and holds out the pure white flower again. You look at him with questioning eyes. He motions for you to take it from him. You grab it hesitantly.

You peer intently at the pure white flower and notice six perfect petals gracing the stem. Kin continues to stand still staring intently at the flower in your hand. He brings his finger to the first petal and lightly traces it.

"Paul the Apostle," he says, then moves his finger to the second petal. "Elijah the Prophet." His finger moves to the third petal. "The woman at the well--the Evangelist." He continues on to the fourth petal. "David the Shepherd," He moves his finger to the fifth petal. "John the Baptist--the Teacher."

Kin places his finger on the sixth petal and stops. You stare at his finger waiting for the last name. Silence follows. You gaze up at Kin and see his eyes are full of tears. He continues to stare down as his tears drip onto the last petal. A holy hush fills the air. Kin begins to weep deeply. You watch as His body slumps to the ground.

The aura of holiness causes tears to form in your eyes. Wind begins to blow more intensely.

"Redeemer…" the word blows as a whisper in the wind. "Redeemer…" the word continues to drift on the wind. Kin sobs harder as the word continues to repeat in the wind. You sink to your knees beside Kin.

"The kindness of Redeemer…" he stutters as his tears continue to fall. "Redeemer's kindness is your transformation!"

Shocked, you gaze intently and say, "What?"

Kin wraps his hand around yours and points to the last petal. "Redeemer…" the word continues to carry on the wind and clouds circle in the sky above. "Redeemer is all five and more."

You grip Kin's hand with yours. "What are you trying to tell me?"

Kin leans in, inches from your face. "The tribes you saw with Redeemer, that is His plan for the last harvest, the training of the saints, and relationship with Him to edify the body of Christ. But they must transform under His guidance, or they will never set aside their pride and work together. Redeemer is all five, therefore He is the One who perfects the saints and edifies them for the work of the ministry." A light flickers in Kin's eyes. "This is His kindness. We find His kindness throughout the holy pages as He transformed Paul, as He equipped Elijah, as He met the woman at the well and called her chosen, as He guided David, and as He enlightened John. You see, they are no different than you and I. They simply experienced the kindness of the Redeemer and allowed Him to transform them--and now it's our turn. It's time for our transformation as we are called by His kindness for the edifying of the body of Christ."

The word "Christ" causes chills to fill your body. "Christ? What do you mean?" you ask insistently.

"Oh, you don't know?" Kin says as He raises His eyebrows.

"Know what?"

"Come, let me show you the ultimate kindness of Redeemer."

Chapter Eleven

The Cross

For the wages of sin is death, but the free gift of God is eternal life in Christ Jesus our Lord.
- Romans 6:23

You follow Kin through the valley as the wind picks up and clouds begin to swirl. You walk quickly behind Kin trying to keep up. Dark storm clouds begin to form as darkness surrounds you.

"Where's Redeemer?" you ask with a shaky voice.

Fear starts to well up within you as the wind picks up even stronger. Its deep whistle pierces your ears. You adjust your helmet to help protect your ears and remove your shield of faith from your back holding it firmly in your hand. In the distance you see a ravine and watch as Kin walks boldly towards it. "There is no way around we must go through" Kin yells over the wind.

Kin leads you down the muddy ravine. As you trudge through ankle deep mud, every step grows heavier and more difficult, as you slip slowly down the ravine.

"Where are we going?" you yell over the wind, but Kin keeps walking without glancing back.

You find your way into the pit of the ravine. The wind begins to blow you left and right causing you to stumble and fall face first into the mud. You pull yourself up and try to wipe the mud from your helmet and breastplate, but it is no use. Discouraged, you cry out and continue trudging through the ravine. You can see Kin's steady stature in front of you, unmoved by the wind. You wipe the mud from your arms and with a determined sigh you continue following Kin.

Heavy rain drops begin to fall as thunder crashes loudly. Kin begins to climb up the other side of the ravine. You strike your shield into the ground to give you leverage as you follow him. Your feet continue to slip under you in the mud. The rain pounds against you and shoots shivers throughout your entire body. The rain falls so heavily you are no longer able to make out Kin. You yell frantically for him as you continue to climb up the side of the ravine. Your legs burn beneath you as you strike your shield at the top and pull yourself out. You use your arms to hoist yourself up and drag your legs from the ravine. You fall onto your stomach and attempt to catch your breath.

Covered in mud, you lift your head and search frantically for Kin. You jump to your feet and place your shield of faith on your back. The rain heavily clouds your vision, but you make out a small figure in the distance and run towards it in your mud caked shoes. A large crash of thunder causes you to falter. You lay on the ground as your breath fills your face shield. You push your body up again, soaked, covered in mud, and continue running towards the small figure. Your armor becomes heavier with the rain. You catch up to Kin and begin to shout, but the storm is too loud to be heard. Kin points in the distance. You make out a large tree on top of a hill. Kin motions for you to follow and begins to run frantically.

The Cross

Fear rushes through your body as your heart pounds within each step. You follow him closely; your legs ache as you run towards the hill. You trip again as mud thickens all around, and you tumble at the foot of the hill. Kin turns around and runs towards you.

"Get up! We must go," he yells above the roar of the storm.

Thunder crashes once again, and you begin to tremble. Exhausted, you let out a wail.

"I can't, I can't, I am too tired."

You sit and bring your legs to your chest and rest in a fetal position as you shake under the rain. Kin reaches for your hand and begins to pull.

"You must! Come on."

You unwrap your legs and grab Kin's hand as he pulls you up. Together you both walk up the slippery mountain. The storm grows more vicious as dark clouds continue to swirl and roll in. You keep your head tucked tightly against your chest and brace yourself against Kin. Your steps are slow and precise. You reach the top of the hill; the rain pours hard around you. Your eyes see the base of a tree and you look upward, then lunge backward, tripping over Kin and plummeting to the ground. You gasp as you see Redeemer nailed to a cross. Refusing to look at His face, your eyes scan down His legs and watch as blood trickles down. You see His hands nailed in place, gushing with blood. You scream and tremble under the weight of what you see. Your eyes move to His chest and sides whipped and bleeding as skin is torn from His bones.

You turn frantically to find Kin, but he is nowhere around. You turn back to Redeemer and notice His shallow breathing and the deep cuts that fill His entire body making Him unrecognizable. You scream out in agony and fall face down in the mud, your entire body sobbing under the weight of anguish. You let out an agonized scream as the rain drenches you and another crash of thunder makes you shudder.

"For you--I did this for you."

The words of Redeemer startle you. With your eyes still closed, pictures begin to flash with the thunder. The thunder crashes and a giant veil tears in two. There's a crack of thunder accompanied with a flash of lightning as screams emanate from hell and the enemy is defeated. A low growl of thunder shakes the ground and sin is removed. There's another crack and more lightning as sickness and sin evaporate. The images stop flashing. You lift up your eyes and catch His strong chin as He musters the strength to hold up His head. You see a crown of thorns dug tightly into His temple forcing blood to stream down His face. You then stare into His eyes of fire. Eyes of kindness and compassion stare back at you. Eyes of mercy and goodness shine for you. Eyes of a savior and the one true Christ burn a hole through you.

"IT IS FINISHED"

The words shatter your heart as you watch His body shake in pain. You sob. His stare continues as He burrows a hole in your heart, perhaps staring at Himself in you. Your body shudders under the weight of His words. Your friend, your guide, hanging there on a cross. His face shakes under the pain.

The Cross

"Thank you, thank you!"

You scream out as you claw at the mud.

Another crash of thunder roars through the air and lightning strikes. Redeemer's eyes still burrowed in yours. You watch as He breathes in and then stops. His head falls heavily against His chest. You shut your eyes and scream again. The storm rages on, the wind howls, and the thunder rolls. Sobs rush through your body.

Suddenly, a holy hush fills the air; the wind stops, and the storm clouds roll away. You lift your head and find the cross has vanished. You are lifted from the ground to your feet by Wind.

You feel a strong hand on your back. Instantly, you turn around and find yourself staring into the eyes of fire-- the eyes of Love. Love reaches out His arms and you fold into His embrace. Words will not come--only sobs. Colors in the sky begin to dance as the clouds part and a ray of sun strikes down on top of you. The warmth of the sun while standing in Love's arms brings ultimate peace. You let go of Love and stare back into His eyes.

"He died for me, and now He is gone!"

You cry out the words and shake violently. Love brings His arms to your shoulders and steadies you.

"Yes, He died for you, so that the veil to the Holy of Holies could be removed, and you could have the chance to stand here in my arms and in my presence. All sin and pain removed. He died for you."

You hang your head. Love reaches for your chin and tilts it up.

Chosen

"Child, not only did He die for you, He rose again for you, to show you His glorious power. You are worthy of it all."

Your eyes widen in amazement as Love turns you around. A ray of sun shifts straight down the valley and shines brightly where Redeemer stands waving. Your heart leaps for joy. Wind races around you in an array of colors; a song from the birds lights up the valley. With an energy you cannot contain, you begin to race down the hill. You lock eyes with Redeemer as you run towards Him. A giant smile spreads across His face. As you draw closer, a sea of colors dances in the sky, and a rainbow shines brightly over His head. Your heart leaps higher in your chest.

"Almost there," Wind yells.

Redeemer opens His arms, and you run straight into His embrace. He engulfs you in a hug picking you up from the ground and twirling you in circles. An enormous laugh leaves your belly as you twirl. The rainbow joins you and engulfs you and Redeemer. The colors begin to dance around you as Redeemer sets you down. He tilts your face upwards, and His eyes shine as they look into yours.

"He has Risen!" yells Wind, as she gushes around you within the rainbow.

The rainbow returns to the sky and standing in its place is Love. He brings His hand to Redeemer's shoulder and pats it lightly. You turn and smile at Love; He smiles back. This glorious scene continues as Love turns from you and locks eyes with Redeemer.

"Son, in you I am well pleased."

The Cross

You watch as a tear slips from Redeemer's eye. He turns and falls into Love's deep embrace. You take a step back as Wind begins to circle around Love and Redeemer. You take a few more steps back, overcome by the glory of this moment. You turn and see Kin a few feet away smiling at Love and Redeemer. You turn and walk towards him. Kin smiles at you.

"I believe it's time I properly introduced myself. I am Kindness. I am the reflection of the Redeemer's gift to you."

You gaze deeply at the old man with kind eyes. A smile spreads across your face,

"Redeemer sent me to show you that He did all of this because of His kindness towards you."

Kindness steps closer to you. A warm smile spreads across your face.

You turn around and see that all your new friends have joined Love and Redeemer. Your first friend, Peace that you met long ago when you journeyed with Love. Peace twirls around Redeemer in an array of colors, and you remember the peace you have felt in your heart since. You watch as Lesson leans in close to Love as she laughs out loud from the kind words He speaks. You turn back to Kindness.

"But where is the woman I met at the waterfall?"

Kindness begins to chuckle and says, "oh, you mean Wind?"

"What?" you shout, "You mean Wind is a person?"

Chosen

You turn back to the circle and watch as Wind transforms into the dark-haired woman with beautiful eyes. She turns in your direction and waves. You wave back with a stunned expression on your face. Kindness continues to laugh. "Love is never without Redeemer or Wind and, friend, neither are you."

Still stunned, you turn back to find your friends and walk to join them. Redeemer looks up at you and with a giant smile.

"Friends," He says turning to Wind, Patience, Lesson, and Kindness, "I want you to meet Chosen."

You stop and look around trying to see who everyone is staring at.

Confused, you blurt out, "Why is everyone staring at me?"

Everyone erupts in laughter. Redeemer steps towards you and grasps your hand.

"*You* are Chosen."

You wrap your arms around Redeemer as He holds you tightly. Wind joins you and wraps her arm around yours as she whispers, "The journey is not over yet!"

Chosen - Study Guide

Soul Expression

Soul Expression is a breakdown of each chapter with correlating scripture of this prophetic journey. This study includes thought-provoking questions to give a deeper and lasting meaning to the essence of an inner healing. Grab your journal and pen as you journey with the Creator of the world through scripture.

Contents

1	The Redeemer	74
2	A Waltz Through Time	78
3	It's Time to Soar	82
4	A Heart that Hungers	86
5	Power of the Mind	90
6	Shield of Faith	97
7	One More Step	102
8	In the Boat	107
9	Helmet of Salvation	112
10	Kindness of Redeemer	118
11	The Cross	123

Chapter One

The Redeemer

Section 1:

I chose to introduce Jesus as Redeemer because the scripture tells us:

> ***In him we have redemption through his blood, the forgiveness of sins, in accordance with the riches of God's grace. - Ephesians 1:7***

What does the word Redemption mean to you?

Do you understand what it means to be redeemed through Christ's blood?

If not, read Ephesians Chapter 1 and ask a spiritual advisor how to decipher the meaning.

Section 2:

As a man, Jesus faced all that we have and yet did not sin. As we grasp the depth of who Redeemer is, we find that He only spoke first what He heard God the Father speak.

> ***For I did not speak on my own, but the Father who sent me commanded me to say all that I have spoken. - John 12:49***

Jesus's entire mission has been to know you and to give you a life of freedom. Can you hear God's voice? Do you speak according to His commands?

Section 3:

Your desire for Jesus grows as you realize that He, too, struggled and cried out to God:

> *About three in the afternoon Jesus cried out in a loud voice, saying, "Eli, Eli, lama sabachthani?" (Which means "My God, my God, why have you forsaken me?) - Matthew 27:46*

Jesus cried out to God when the sin of the world had fallen on Him. This was a declaration as God turned His back on that sin and Jesus successfully defeated sin for you and me. Because of what Jesus did, God will never turn His back on us because sin has been defeated.

List three ways you can relate to Jesus.

His Redemption for you is so intimate that He made a way for kindness to become a part of you.

What does the word repentance mean to you?

How does repentance look in your life?

Repentance not only means to ask for forgiveness but to turn from your sin.

Section 4:

The intent of the journey in this book is for us to let our walls down and experience Jesus.

> *But the Lord is faithful, and he will strengthen you and protect you from the evil one. - 2 Thessalonians 3:3*

Ask Jesus to show you how He is faithful.

We then see that Redeemer wants to bring joy back into your life.

> *You make known to me the path of life; you will fill me with joy in your presence with eternal pleasures at your right hand. - Psalm 16:11*

Can you find joy amongst chaos?

Can you tell the difference in your heart when you have joy?

Take a piece of paper and through scripture write down Jesus's character when He displays joy.

We begin to see that we are chosen--a royal priesthood—and through Christ we are destined and called by name.

> *But you are a chosen people, a royal priesthood, a holy nation, God's special possession, that you may declare the praises of him who called you out of darkness into his wonderful light. - 1 Peter 2:9*

What does it mean to be chosen by God?

How did Jesus make that a reality for you?

Section 5:

You are then introduced to the presence of Jesus and begin the journey once again.

> *Where can I go from your Spirit? Where can I flee from your presence? - Psalm 139:7*

As you realize you are back in the presence of Love, your heart leaps with joy and excitement. You are introduced to Redeemer and watch as colors dance in His eyes.

Fixing our eyes on Jesus, the pioneer and perfecter of faith. For the joy set before him he endured the cross, scorning its shame, and sat down at the right hand of the throne of God. - Hebrews 12:2

Jesus is the perfecter of our faith, sitting at the right hand of the Father. Though they are one, their characteristics are different.

List 3 attributes of God then list 3 attributes of Jesus.

Write a letter to Redeemer thanking and acknowledging what He did for you on the cross.

Chapter Two

A Waltz Through Time

Section 1:

As you begin this journey with Redeemer, you must first remember the journey with Love, your first love passion. We must never abandon our first love.

> **Yet I hold this against you: You have forsaken the love you had at first. - Revelation 2:4**

> **Because of the increase of wickedness, the love of most will grow cold. - Matthew 24:12**

Who should be your first love passion above all else?

How could the worlds pain cause you to grow cold to God's love?

As the journey begins you find yourself step in step with Love reliving what He did for you in the book *Loved*.

> **Let your eyes look straight ahead; fix your gaze directly before you. - Proverbs 4:25**

As you journey into the past, why is it important to keep looking ahead?

We are "overcomers" by our testimony. It is great to look back and see how far we have come but we mustn't stay there and get stuck.

Section 2:

Memories of renewal bring sweetness to our mind. We must not get lost in only the hard parts of our story but also the sweetness along the way.

> **See to it that no one falls short of the grace of God and that no bitter root grows up to cause trouble and defile many. - Hebrews 12:15**

A bitter heart can stop the process of renewal. You can become stuck in a pattern of anger and bitterness if you don't allow the process of forgiveness to guide you.

Ask God to show you any bitterness you have been carrying.
Surrender the bitterness and allow the renewal to come.

Do you trust that God has removed the bitterness and brought renewal?

Section 3:

A common theme throughout the book is our need to be rescued and reminded of our worth. It's important that you settle in your heart that you are chosen not because of anything you have done but because of what Jesus had done for you.

> **For it is by grace you have been saved, through faith—and this is not from yourselves, it is the gift of God— not by works, so that no one can boast. - Ephesians 2:8-9**

Have you ever struggled with the thought that you are unworthy?

What are some ways you overcome these thoughts?
Quote the scripture above over and over in your mind and heart. Decide to trust that the gift of God is yours and there is nothing you can do to earn it, just simply accept it.

Section 4:

Throughout the book you will be given the chance to glimpse into the holiness and sovereignty of not only Love but Redeemer. We must continue to revere the King of Kings.

> ***There is no one holy like the Lord; there is no one besides you; there is no Rock like our God. - 1 Samuel 2:2***

Spend some time in reverence for the King. Think of His power and might. Pause and ponder His goodness.

Section 5:

You once again are reminded of Love's goodness as He reassures you that "He is always near and never far." It can be scary going on a new adventure, but when we trust in God the Father as He guides us into Jesus the Son, our trust must be magnified.

> ***And a voice from heaven said, "This is my Son, whom I love; with him I am well pleased." - Matthew 3:17***

Take a moment and meditate on the goodness of God the Father, and the kindness of Jesus the Son.

As you embrace Redeemer you notice His features are different from Love's. Perhaps this is to teach us to desire what comes from the inside instead of the outside.

Do you naturally look at the hearts of people?

Ask God to give you His eyes so you are not caught up in fleshly attraction.

> ***Now the main point of what we are saying is this: We do have such a high priest, who sat down at the right hand of the throne of the Majesty in heaven. - Hebrews 8:1***

Allow the word *Majesty* to fall on your lips as your trust in Him deepens.

Where is your trust placed when your life gets shaken?

List 3 ways you can deepen your trust in Jesus.

The sound of Redeemer's laughter is like medicine to your soul.

> ***A cheerful heart is good medicine, but a crushed spirit dries up the bones. - Proverbs 17:22***

Write a letter to yourself from a place of joy, encouraging yourself to take a step of faith in your new identity in Christ.

Chapter Three

It's Time to Soar

Section 1:

The smell of sweet honey fills your nostrils. You feel refreshed from a great night's sleep and ready to take on the world.

> ***But you would be fed with the finest of wheat; with honey from the rock, I would satisfy you. - Psalm 81:16***

Have you ever felt satisfied by what Christ has to offer you?

Imagine a feeling so refreshing that your entire body is at ease breathing in the sweetness of Jesus.

With this thought in mind, allow your body to relax and picture this sweet scene in your mind. What do you see, hear, smell, taste, and touch?

Section 2:

The feeling of Redeemer brings a gentle peace as you watch Him make you the perfect pancake. Hungry and curious, you ask what it is, and, to your delight, Redeemer says, "Taste and see." This is our command to taste and see that all things are good when we take refuge in the Lord.

> ***Taste and see that the Lord is good; blessed is the one who takes refuge in him. - Psalm 34:8***

It's easy to recognize the things in this life that we see as good, but what about things that are good for us that we don't necessarily like?

Do you trust God's goodness as He leads you through growth that doesn't feel good?

How can you choose to feel God's goodness in all circumstances?

Section 3:

The soothing taste of honey brings great joy, and even deeper joy comes as Redeemer introduces you to living water to quench your soul.

> *But whoever drinks the water I give them will never thirst. Indeed, the water I give them will become in them a spring of water welling up to eternal life. - John 4:14*

Are you consumed with the water of this world or are you tapping into the eternal living water?

So often we are afraid to soar for fear of falling or failing. Faith requires one jump, even when it feels like we are free falling. If we will just take a moment to remember who is in the air with us, our body will settle, and we will see Jesus was always holding on.

> *Like an eagle that stirs up its nest and hovers over its young, that spreads its wings to catch them and carries them aloft. - Deuteronomy 32:11*

> *Does the hawk take flight by your wisdom and spread its wings toward the south? - Job 36:26*

In what areas of your life is God asking you to jump?

In what areas of your life is God asking you to soar?

Through it all can you see Jesus clutching your hand and never letting go?

Section 4:

It is through the wisdom of God that all things are directed. Surrender to Him and take that leap of faith; you just might soar.

Once you learn to soar the goal is to mimic Jesus. Let Him be your guide for how you live your life.

> **Whoever claims to live in him must live as Jesus did. - 1 John 2:6**
>
> **To this you were called, because Christ suffered for you, leaving you an example, that you should follow in his steps. - 1 Peter 2:21**

How can you follow the example of Jesus in your daily life?

Make a list of your favorite stories of Jesus throughout the Bible and study what He did and how he acted. How can you apply that to your own life?

Section 5:

The journey of living as a chosen child of God is the journey of letting go. This means letting go of your wants, desires, ideals, and agenda and surrendering truly to the King of kings.

> **I have been crucified with Christ and I no longer live, but Christ lives in me. The life I now live in the body, I live by faith in the Son of God, who**

loved me and gave himself for me. - Galatians 2:20

The journey is not promised too always be sweet. Often, we must be cracked open to expose what is on the inside. However, God is gracious, and the journey will be life to your bones.

What are you going to change today so you can soar?

Chapter Four

A Heart That Hungers

Section 1:

The picture unfolds as you sense the deep urgency of this encounter. We find throughout the Bible that Jesus was tempted three times. We, too, are tempted with those same things.

> ***Then Jesus was led by the Spirit into the wilderness to be tempted by the devil. After fasting forty days and forty nights, he was hungry. The tempter came to him and said, "If you are the Son of God, tell these stones to become bread." Jesus answered, "It is written: Man shall not live on bread alone, but on every word that comes from the mouth of God." - Matthew 4:1-4***

Temptation 1: Hunger/satisfaction.

How is this a temptation in your life?

How do you see this temptation causing issues?

Fearful on the journey, the forest around you is dark and the noises are new. You feel fear begin to take over. Redeemer steadies your heart as He encourages you to trust the process.

> ***Trust in the Lord with all your heart and lean not on your own understanding; in all your ways***

> *submit to him, and he will make your paths straight. - Proverbs 3:5-6*

Have you ever felt like you were in a confusing process?

How did you handle that feeling?

Leaning on our own understanding can cause deeper confusion. We must submit to the process of God and His ways as He makes our paths straight.

As you settle in the clearing, you watch Redeemer find a piece of wood filled with your accomplishments--the things you did for Him. You watch sadness cross His face as you look at Him confused.

> *Not everyone who says to me, 'Lord, Lord,' will enter the kingdom of heaven, but only the one who does the will of my Father who is in heaven. Many will say to me on that day, "Lord, Lord, did we not prophesy in your name and in your name drive out demons and, in your name, perform many miracles?" Then I will tell them plainly, "I never knew you. Away from me, you evildoers!" - Matthew 7:21-23*

Section 2:

God is not impressed with what we can do for Him. Success is tempting because it makes us feel good. We fall into temptation when we try to make it about what we can do for God. God is all-powerful. He wants a relationship with you, not a person who can *do* for Him. Yes, our gifts are important but not above our relationship with Him.

What areas of your life are only about success?

Soul Expression

Is what you do for God more important than your relationship with Him?

As Redeemer shares His temptation of hunger, you realize your temptation is a deep hunger to be liked by the world, to be accepted, to accomplish much for the approval of others, and to succeed so you can prove your worth.

Doing well in life is only wrong when we put any of these things before God.

> **So do not worry, saying, "What shall we eat?" or "What shall we drink?" or "What shall we wear?" For the pagans run after all these things, and your heavenly Father knows that you need them. But seek first his kingdom and his righteousness, and all these things will be given to you as well. - Matthew 6:31-33**

What are you putting before God?

How do you see yourself in Jesus's temptation?

Section 3:

Ask God to give you peace as you surrender any idol you have put before Him.

Receive His forgiveness and ask Him to show you His true Kingdom. As you advance in the call He has given, you will be filled and will not seek success outside of your relationship with Him.

God is quick to forgive as we surrender and repent. He picks up our broken pieces and makes beauty out of our pain.

When temptation comes, we must not give in to its clutches and must recognize the traps of ungodly success.

What are three ways you can end the drive for ungodly success in your life and remove the pride that has taken root?

Section 4:

True success comes when we include God in all that we do and give Him the honor. Embrace His goodness in your life, live a life of love, and keep seeing the truth of the idols in your life.

> ***Take delight in the Lord, and he will give you the desires of your heart. - Psalm 37:4***

How are you using your gifts to delight in the Lord?

Ask God to fill your heart with the truth He has for you.

Write down the dreams that God has for you as you succeed in Him.

As we journey through the hard realities of uncovering our heart's intentions, God always brings us into rest. Rest in Him and know that He has good things for you, but nothing should ever be put before Him.

Write a letter to Jesus letting Him know he has your heart, success, and ambitions for the Kingdom of Heaven.

Chapter Five

Power of the Mind

Section 1:

When we are first confronted with the reality that Redeemer is gone, we begin to panic thinking that He is disappointed and no longer with us on the journey. The second temptation begins.

Then the devil took him to the holy city and had him stand on the highest point of the temple. "If you are the Son of God," he said, "throw yourself down. For it is written: He will command his angels concerning you and they will lift you up in their hands, so that you will not strike your foot against a stone." Jesus answered him, "It is also written: Do not put the Lord your God to the test." - Matthew 4:5-7

Temptation 2: Testing God/prove who you are

How is this a temptation in your life?

How do you see this temptation causing issues?

Three things to remember if you feel like a disappointment and want to prove yourself to others:
1. God doesn't remember your past sin.
2. God's love isn't dependent on your actions.
3. God sees the whole story.

Discouragement and doubt prey on those who feel lost and sad. It comes on the heels of depression and anxiety causing us to lose sight of what God offers us.

> *He gives strength to the weary and increases the power of the weak. Even youths grow tired and weary, and young men stumble and fall; but those who hope in the Lord will renew their strength. They will soar on wings like eagles; they will run and not grow weary; they will walk and not be faint. - Isaiah 40:29-31*

What are signs you are becoming discouraged?

How is doubt and discouragement different?

What does it mean when God says He gives strength to the weary?

Share a time when you were weary, and God strengthened you. Remind yourself of His goodness.

Section 2:

As the snake begins to test you, you respond hesitantly trying to get away from him. But his words are enticing, his eyes intriguing, and his points seemingly of value. This is what deceit looks like. Do not fall for the schemes of the enemy or the way he twists truth and scripture.

> *Dear friends, do not believe every spirit, but test the spirits to see whether they are from God, because many false prophets have gone out into the world. - 1 John 4:1*

> *The great dragon was hurled down—that ancient serpent called the devil, or Satan, who leads the*

> *whole world astray. He was hurled to the earth, and his angels with him. - Revelation 12:9*

What does deception look like?

Past or present—in what areas of your life have you been deceived?

We overcome deception by renewing our mind to the Word and testing the spirits to see whether they are from God. God brings life, and life more abundantly. Test each spirit against the knowledge of God according to the Bible. Rebuke any deception and repent for what you have allowed into your life.

*Note: It is helpful to talk with spiritual advisors about deception, glean from their wisdom, and make sure their teaching is biblically sound.

Section 3:

When deception strikes, we are filled with despair and hope is deferred. If we allow it, this will lead to deep depression and suffering as we grasp at anything that comes our way, ultimately finding ourselves in a deep hole questioning the goodness of Redeemer.

> *At one time we too were foolish, disobedient, deceived and enslaved by all kinds of passions and pleasures. We lived in malice and envy, being hated and hating one another. But when the kindness and love of God our Savior appeared, he saved us, not because of righteous things we had done, but because of his mercy. He saved us through the washing of rebirth and renewal by the Holy Spirit, whom he poured out on us gen-*

erously through Jesus Christ our Savior, so that, having been justified by his grace, we might become heirs having the hope of eternal life. - Titus 3:3-7

Can you think of a time when your heart was deceived and led to depression?

Did you fall prey to thinking God isn't who He said He was?

Reread the scripture above. Though you have allowed your emotions and deceit to lead you astray, God's kindness through His Son led you back to His Grace. Lay your head on His chest and listen to the thumping of His heart. Let your broken soul be healed in that place.

Section 4:

As you suddenly realize you are sitting in the presence of the Redeemer, your body settles. Though anger and sorrow fill your heart as you cry out that He has left you, His presence is sweet and comforting. Redeemer jumps in the hole next to you and sits in the mud. Jesus is with you on the journey ready to sit with you.

The Lord is close to the brokenhearted and saves those who are crushed in spirit. - Psalm 34:18

Jesus is not afraid of your pain, sorrow, or anger.

You are called a son and daughter, and He sits with you in your pain but doesn't want you to stay there.

What is stopping you from stepping into freedom? Feel your anger and sorrow and express it with Him. He is ready to listen.

You soon realize that Redeemer never left you, even when it feels this way. We must look outside of ourselves and there we will find His presence. Redeemer tenderly cares for our wounds, bringing healing and freedom.

> *Heal me, Lord, and I will be healed; save me and I will be saved, for you are the one I praise. - Jeremiah 17:14*

Jesus is the ultimate healer of our emotional and physical wounds. Ask Him to reveal to you the places of your heart that need to be healed. Allow Him to bring that healing to you.

Section 5:

As Redeemer begins to reveal to you the schemes of the tempter, it becomes obvious that you fell prey to his lies feeling the need to prove your love for Redeemer. Love is an action not a word; it is displayed in your relationship with Him. The tempter will always come with doubt, trying to throw you off, and to convince you that Jesus's redemption was not enough--but we know the truth.

> *Jesus asked the boy's father, "How long has he been like this?" "From childhood," he answered. "It has often thrown him into fire or water to kill him. But if you can do anything, take pity on us and help us." "'If you can'?" said Jesus. "Everything is possible for one who believes." Immediately the boy's father exclaimed, "I do believe; help me overcome my unbelief!" - Mark 9:21-24*

> *Who gave himself for our sins to rescue us from the present evil age, according to the will of our God and Father. - Galatians 1:4*

When doubt comes, ask Jesus to help you overcome your disbelief.

Jesus came to rescue us from the present age because that is the will of the Father.

Ask God to reveal areas of doubt in your life.

What is God's will for you?

Section 6:

The key to confronting the enemy is to keep Redeemer close. Focus on your relationship with Him, stay unified, and make Him a part of your everyday life.

> *Submit yourselves, then, to God. Resist the devil, and he will flee from you. - James 4:7*

> *And whatever you do, whether in word or deed, do it all in the name of the Lord Jesus, giving thanks to God the Father through him. - Colossians 3:17*

In what areas have you stood firm against the enemy?

In everything you do, make Jesus a part of it. How does this manifest in your life?

The snake had the leverage to bite you because you gave into His lies and doubted the truth. Stand steadfast in the truth and reject the lies. Cling to the truth of the Word of God. Stay focused on the eyes of Jesus and allow Him to pull you out of your hole every single time.

> *Set your minds on things above, not on earthly things. - Colossians 3:2*

Soul Expression

Put on the full armor of God, so that you can take your stand against the devil's schemes.
- Ephesians 6:11

Write your own guide to what a relationship with Jesus looks like to you.

Ask Him to reveal His unique love to you

Write what He showed you.

Chapter Six

Shield of Faith

Section 1:

You soon find yourself out of the wilderness and in the clearing with joy on your side. You are distracted by curiosity as you begin your journey towards the busyness of the next season. Setting you up for the third temptation,

> *Again, the devil took him to a very high mountain and showed him all the kingdoms of the world and their splendor. "All this I will give you," he said, "if you will bow down and worship me." Jesus said to him, "Away from me, Satan! For it is written: Worship the Lord your God, and serve him only." Then the devil left him, and angels came and attended him. - Matthew 4:5-7*

Temptation 3: Devotion to God/power

How is this a temptation in your life?

How do you see this temptation causing issues?

How distracted are we in this life? Do we notice the hustle and bustle? Do we stop when we notice the old beggar or the well-dressed man? Who captures our attention? Do we keep our heads down and refuse to engage? Or do we fight back pushing our way to the center to gain what we perceive as our rightful place in line?

Do nothing from selfish ambition or conceit, but in humility count others more significant than yourselves. - Philippians 2:3

What do you find captures the majority of your attention?

How do you care for others?

Are you highly distracted by the hustle and bustle of this world?

Section 2:

Once we are knocked down to others' levels, that is often when we begin to notice them. As you are pushed from the stand of gold coins and others who can afford to make that purchase, you find yourself in the dirt next to the old beggar. She informs you that the least of these are the greatest in the Redeemer's Kingdom, and states that He takes good care of her, but how can that be?

The King will reply, "Truly I tell you, whatever you did for one of the least of these brothers and sisters of mine, you did for me." - Matthew 25:40

How often do we judge others based on what they have and call it God's blessing on their lives?

Do you judge others based on their appearance?

How does God view this Kingdom?

What does Matthew 25:40 tell us?

Section 3:

Many times, while we are on our journey, we have questions that do not get answered. We want to make sense of everything that happens, but some answers do not come until later.

Once you reach the outskirts of the forest, still curious about the old beggar, you find Redeemer sitting under an Oak Tree.

Why an Oak Tree?

The Oak tree is one of the most loved trees in the world-- and with good reason. It's a symbol of strength, morale, resistance, and knowledge.

> *That person is like a tree planted by streams of water, which yields its fruit in season and whose leaf does not wither whatever they do prospers. - Psalm 1:3*

You recognize the old beggar now standing tall and exquisite as her eyes shine with fire. She is Lesson, and she hands you the shield of faith.

> *In addition to all this, take up the shield of faith, with which you can extinguish all the flaming arrows of the evil one. - Ephesians 6:16*

Section 4:

We are so consumed with our own journey that we often don't recognize what Jesus is doing in others. We put ourselves up higher due to ambitious pride. This is where faith comes in, faith that Redeemer is the one who takes each of us on a journey. He takes our hearts into His hands and shapes us to be more like Him if we are willing. We must never judge another; we have no idea what journey they are truly on.

> ***Do not judge, or you too will be judged. For in the same way you judge others, you will be judged, and with the measure you use, it will be measured to you. - Matthew 7:1-2***

We all labor, we all struggle, but we must never become haughty and compare ourselves to others.

What is one way you can choose to be more like Jesus every day?

What are some consistent judgements you have carried your whole life?

How are you pursuing help for these issues?

Section 5:

Tears fall from your eyes as you realize the material things are simply that--*things*. They bring no eternal value. It is God and God alone who deserves our complete devotion and our utmost praise. Do not worship the things He can do for you or the blessings He gives you. Worship Him simply because He is worthy.

> ***I will exalt you, my God the King; I will praise your name for ever and ever. - Psalm 145:1***

> ***You are worthy, our Lord and God, to receive glory and honor and power, for you created all things, and by your will they were created and have their being. - Revelation 4:11***

God is able and willing. He wants to bless you beyond measure but, above all else, our desire should be *Him*.

Do you struggle with separating God and God's blessing for you?

If so, where is that struggle rooted?

Ask God to reveal His heart to you and remember that God's voice always lines up with His Word; it's His basis of truth.

Once you realize God's love for you and His desire for you, then you can't help but abound in every good work.

Write a letter to yourself about how you see God's blessings in your life. Choose to see how His nature calls you worthy. Be patient and kind. Then give yourself permission to let go of the materialistic focus in your life and move into complete trust in God as your source. Encourage yourself to step into the destiny God has for you and leave your idols behind. Refuse to bow to them ever again.

Chapter Seven

One More Step

Section 1:

Once again, while looking for Redeemer, you know not to fear. He has a specific journey in mind for you. As you follow in His footsteps, you find a staircase going down the cliff and step onto it boldly.

> ***Direct my footsteps according to your word; let no sin rule over me. - Psalm 119:133***

Take a moment to pause and ponder, what areas of your life have you been chasing?

What areas is God asking you to surrender for a season?

Have you ever found yourself in a season of fear, where it feels like darkness surrounds you, and the only thing you can see is the next step in front of you?

Section 2:

Panic sets in as shaky step after shaky step confirms the reality that you are walking down an open staircase in complete darkness, and if you fall you will drop to the canyon floor.

> ***I will give you every place where you set your foot, as I promised Moses. - Joshua 1:3***

You must remember that Jesus already walked the path we are on. The trail is worn with His footsteps. When fear sets in and we become shaky under the knowledge of that one wrong step, remember the path is worn and Jesus will be your guide.

Think over the past and write down times when you know Jesus walked before you.

Hindsight is 20/20. We must trust the path that Jesus has set for us. Though the night is dark, joy comes in the morning.

Section 3:

The fresh air of Wind whips lightly across your face giving you renewed strength and breath and encouraging you to continue on.

"Endure my friend. You must keep going--not quickly though. Try going slowly." The words from Wind are gentle. We try so often to rush through hard, dark seasons. We want to move quickly, but it causes our hearts more damage. God is with us always, but rest is crucial and slowing down and learning will cause your heart much freedom in this season.

> ***Establish my footsteps in Your word, And do not let any iniquity have dominion over me. - Psalm 119:133***

When fear and *what ifs* ring loudly, we must take a step with Faith and shout: "BUT GOD."
What is one area in your life that has frozen you in your tracks? Ask the Holy Spirit to reveal the truth to you about this situation.

According to scripture, what is God's truth for you?

Section 4:

Step after step, your body settles into the rhythm of the motion. With the encouraging words of Wind, you find your footing and realize you are halfway there. Encouragement fills you up as you begin to trust yourself once again.

> *I remain confident of this: I will see the goodness of the Lord in the land of the living. Wait for the Lord; be strong and take heart and wait for the Lord. - Psalm 27:13-14*

Is Jesus the source of your confidence as you settle into step with Him?

Have you made Jesus a divine portion in every area of your life?

What areas do you want Jesus to come in and cleanse?

Write a letter to Jesus asking Him to cleanse every area of your life and to remove fear, as He establishes your path and guides you with knowledge that He in YOU is greater than He in the world.

Section 5:

The steps continue to narrow until you find yourself plummeting down with only a moment to save yourself. With the sound of water providing hope, you stand and continue to walk cautiously and slowly as the stairs keep narrowing.

> *For though the righteous fall seven times, they rise again, but the wicked stumble when calamity strikes. - Proverbs 24:16*

Though you may fall, do you find the courage to get back up?

Allow God to give you the courage to fight again, to get back up again, and do so with the confidence that Jesus is cheering you on.

Write down three things that have knocked you down and how you are choosing to get back up and fight.

Section 4:

As you run to the waterfall and across the rocks, you are met with a reflection of yourself that is dirty and exhausted. You watch as the dirty water follows you as you make it to the waterfall and are beat down by the strength of the water. With cuts on your legs and a weary body, you finally make it to the rock and peer behind.

> *Therefore, we do not lose heart. Though outwardly we are wasting away, yet inwardly we are being renewed day by day. For our light and momentary troubles are achieving for us an eternal glory that far outweighs them all. So, we fix our eyes not on what is seen, but on what is unseen, since what is seen is temporary, but what is unseen is eternal. - 2 Corinthians 4:16-18*

Despite your circumstances, do not lose heart, do not allow yourself to waste away. God has so much for you. You must simply stand and fight even if that means doing so a bit more slowly!

As we close out this chapter, the experience of healing is the focus as you meet the woman. Healing always comes, renewal always comes, but it requires patience on our part as we endure with Redeemer as our guide.

Friend, it's time to dance in the waterfall. To cast away all of your burdens and pain as the refreshing water cleanses you and you laugh out loud as joy fills your weary bones. There is nothing too dirty for Jesus to make clean. One patient step at a time leads us to beautiful places.

Chapter Eight

In the Boat

Section 1:

After a long journey we are always brought back to a season of stillness and a season of peace, allowing our armor to be readjusted and to dwell on the things we have been taught in the past season.

> *Do not gloat over me, my enemy! Though I have fallen, I will rise. Though I sit in darkness, the Lord will be my light. - Micah 7:8*

This type of peace comes from the eyes of Jesus and time spent in His presence. Jesus is always ready for an adventure. He is your guide, and there is sure to be fun and lessons learned along the way.

Have you ever been on an adventure with Jesus? Take some time and plan out a day, just you and Him. Write down three things you can do together.

As your eyes catch a glimpse of your reflection, you find it to be clear and whole. This is what time in Redeemer's presence does. We must never take Him for granted; abiding in Jesus is the secret to life.

> *Anyone who runs ahead and does not continue in the teaching of Christ does not have God; whoever continues in the teaching has both the Father and the Son. - 2 John 1:9*

Section 2:

As the trip continues, excitement to go fishing sets in until you realize you are not good at it. Embarrassed and ashamed, you try to hide your mistake from Redeemer. Unfazed, He coaches you in patience and lets you know He is proud of you just the way you are. How often does Jesus ask something of us even though we are not very good at it?

When have you stepped out recently and didn't like the outcome?

Are you bold in trying new things?

Trust that Jesus will equip and guide you, as you step out with patience in what He has called you to do.

Many of us desire to serve God but become discouraged when people don't respond the way we anticipate. Being a fisher of men is costly and requires the guidance of Jesus.

> ***"Come, follow me," Jesus said, "and I will send you out to fish for people." - Matthew 4:19***

We must remember that there is no requirement on us to achieve. The feeling of needing to gain something is a spirit of performance. We don't gain God's love by leading others to Christ. We simply give out of the outpour that was first given to us.

Do you struggle with performance?

Are you trying to gain God's love?

What would it look like to step out and serve God because of what He did for you and not because you must earn something?

Section 3:

Frustrated that Redeemer did not answer your question but instead instructed you to continue fishing, you cast the line forgetting to use patience. The line tangles; Redeemer does not become angry. He simply untangles your line and places it back in your hand.

> *But when the kindness and love of God our Savior appeared, he saved us, not because of righteous things we had done, but because of his mercy. He saved us through the washing of rebirth and renewal by the Holy Spirit, whom he poured out on us generously through Jesus Christ our Savior. - Titus 3:4-6*

When we don't hear an answer to our exact question, we often fall prey to frustration.

Jesus is not angry by your outbursts; He simply comes in and cleans up your mess and encourages you to keep going.

What does this kind of love and redemption mean to your heart?

Section 4:

After the perfect cast is thrown, joy races through your heart. Redeemer removes the tear from your cheek and tells you the secret to the question you asked: Abiding in Him.

> *Since then, you have been raised with Christ, set your hearts on things above, where Christ is, seated at the right hand of God. Set your minds on things above, not on earthly things. For you*

> *died, and your life is now hidden with Christ in God. - Colossians 3:1-3*

What do the words "Abiding in Me" mean to you?

Write an expression of love to Jesus Christ for His divine example of love as He paid the ultimate price for you to abide in Him and be saved.

As Redeemer shares the secret, He says, "You are worth loving, you are worth protecting, you are seen, you will only know this truth by abiding in me."

> *But God demonstrates his own love for us in this: While we were still sinners, Christ died for us. - Romans 5:8*

> *...and through him to reconcile to himself all things, whether things on earth or things in heaven, by making peace through his blood, shed on the cross.- Colossians 1:20*

Section 5:

Through the blood of Christ you are protected and seen. His spirit can dwell in you now as you follow Jesus as your peace and as your guide, and as you accept the Holy Spirit.

What has God taught you through this chapter?

The renewal takes place within the resistance and the endurance.

> *Take my yoke upon you and learn from me, for I am gentle and humble in heart, and you will find rest for your souls. - 2 Corinthians 4:16*

> *Let us not become weary in doing good, for at the proper time we will reap a harvest if we do not give up. - Galatians 6:9*

> *Not only so, but we also glory in our sufferings, because we know that suffering produces perseverance; perseverance, character; and character, hope. - Romans 5:3-4*

We must walk assuredly knowing that abiding requires surrender and a simple proclamation that Jesus is King, and His blood is enough.

> *For the life of a creature is in the blood, and I have given it to you to make atonement for yourselves on the altar; it is the blood that makes atonement for one's life. - Leviticus 17:11*

> *How blessed are those who keep justice, who practice righteousness at all times! - Psalm 106:3*

Reread the end of Chapter 8 and describe the encounter with Redeemer in your own words. How will you apply these scriptures in your own life?

Through the scriptures and in your own words, write down what patience and resilience have to do with abiding in Christ.

Choose to live a life of abiding. In the stillness next to Him.

Chapter Nine

Helmet of Salvation

Section 1:

Renewed by the fishing trip, you find yourself back in the boat.

> *The Lord is my shepherd, I lack nothing. He makes me lie down in green pastures, he leads me beside quiet waters, he refreshes my soul. He guides me along the right paths for his name's sake. - Psalm 23:1-3*

Next to the still waters or within the valley you will find Him. Next to Redeemer you race as birds fly overhead and the deer dance through the valley.

> *Until the day breaks, and the shadows flee, turn, my beloved, and be like a gazelle or like a young stag on the rugged hills. - Song of Solomon 2:17*

Why Deer? Deer serve as a reminder for people to maintain their surefootedness and devotion to God amidst the perils they can face on Earth.

Why Birds? Many of the birds in the Bible represent the best in us – what's noble – pointing us towards the best versions of ourselves.

How does creation speak to you?

Section 2:

As you follow Redeemer into a small split in the canyon, you are handed a pickaxe and instructed to strike. At first you are filled with energy, but after a few strikes and not much progress you grow tired.

> **Take the staff, and you and your brother Aaron gather the assembly together. Speak to that rock before their eyes and it will pour out its water. You will bring water out of the rock for the community so they and their livestock can drink. - Numbers 20:8-9**

Only God can show us our purpose and instruct our next move. Even when we don't understand, we must keep striking the rock that is blocking our way because eventually water will gush out.

Why a pickaxe? A pickaxe is a symbol representing hard work, creation, and steadfastness.

What has God instructed you to do in this season? How are you being steadfast in that instruction?

Section 3:

After you have tried to make a dent in the wall, your body gives up and you quit. Redeemer takes your spot and finishes swinging the pickaxe until the perfect hole is complete. Isn't this a picture of Christ? He took your place on the cross. He died for you so you would not face eternal punishment for sin. He stepped in and completed what it took for your salvation. He then called you to receive the helmet as if you were the one who worked for it. This is the work of Jesus; this is the power of your salvation.

> *Salvation is found in no one else, for there is no other name under heaven given to mankind by which we must be saved. - Acts 4:12*

What have you been striking at that you need to give to God?

Seeing is not always believing. Ask Jesus to show you what rocks He has removed for your personal circumstances.

What did salvation do for you - "It's a physical representation of the deliverance from harm, ruin, loss, and sin. The ultimate price that was paid for you. The helmet protects your mind from the confusion and schemes of the enemy. The helmet also supports the crest. The helmet represents your rank in my army, as a friend and child. Your salvation grants you the position to walk in the love, power, and authority granted to you through my sacrifice."

> *Take the helmet of salvation and the sword of the Spirit, which is the word of God. - Ephesians 6:17*

For without salvation, we are left in the darkness, tormented and subject to fear. With Salvation we are called a child of God. Salvation is a gift; it cannot be earned. The gift was bought and paid for through the sacrifice of Jesus.

> *He has saved us and called us to a holy life—not because of anything we have done but because of his own purpose and grace. This grace was given us in Christ Jesus before the beginning of time. - 2 Timothy 1:9*

What does "living in the light" mean?

Section 4:

Redeemer places the helmet on your head signifying that He has chosen you and sees you as His. The gift cannot be obtained on its own; it comes with a relationship with Jesus. Position and authority come with guidance and wisdom. Jesus is your guide and your source of all wisdom.

> *I have loved you with an everlasting love; therefore, I have continued my faithfulness to you. - Jeremiah 31:3*

> *Whoever claims to live in him must live as Jesus did. - 1 John 2:6*

You are loved and wanted with an everlasting love; it will never end. You are not alone and never will be when you make Jesus the Lord of your life.

As you learn to live in Jesus, refer to the scriptures and watch Jesus' life on display.

As we wear our helmet of Salvation with confidence, Redeemer reminds us that the enemy now sees us as Jesus. Jesus defeated Satan when He went to the cross, so when Satan tries to harass us just remind him who you truly are by flipping down your shield. When you do this, you are proclaiming that you are a child of God, you carry the price of salvation, and Jesus is on your side.

> *The one who does what is sinful is of the devil, because the devil has been sinning from the beginning. The reason the Son of God appeared was to destroy the devil's work. - 1 John 3:8*

> *Jesus replied, "What is impossible with man is possible with God." - Luke 18:27*

What gives you hope?

Why should you keep the face shield flipped down?

> *The Lord is my strength and shield. I trust him with all my heart. He helps me, and my heart is filled with joy. I burst out in songs of thanksgiving. - Psalm 28:7*

> *And one of the elders saith unto me, "Weep not: behold, the Lion of the tribe of Judah, the Root of David, hath prevailed to open the book, and to loose the seven seals thereof." - Revelation 5:5*

Section 5:

There is only one permitted to open the scrolls; there is only one who is the author of salvation, and He calls you friend. Run to him and within His presence you will find the answer; you will find hope; you will be saved.

Take time to imagine the helmet of salvation and what Jesus did for you. Write down what you see.

You have gained much from the journey with Redeemer, but your armor is by far the most valuable. Never forget the armor that is yours to wear and the power and significance in wearing it.

> *Finally, be strong in the Lord and in his mighty power. Put on the full armor of God, so that you can take your stand against the devil's schemes. For our struggle is not against flesh and blood, but against the rulers, against the authorities, against the powers of this dark world and against the spiritual forces of evil in the heavenly realms. Therefore, put on the full armor of God, so that*

when the day of evil comes, you may be able to stand your ground, and after you have done everything, to stand. - Ephesians 6:10-13

What does the armor signify to you?

What armor feels comfortable?

What armor are you learning to wear properly?

Chapter Ten

Kindness of Redeemer

Section 1:

Once again you are on a journey with Redeemer, but this time it feels different. Redeemer is stern and on a mission. He acts different from His normal joyful and carefree character. You watch as the business of the tribes unfold as each tribe completes their specific assignment in great detail.

> ***Many are the plans in a person's heart, but it is the Lord's purpose that prevails. - Proverbs 19:21***

We are busy by nature; not only is it wired into our DNA but also into our culture. We find ourselves so focused on our specific endeavors that we forget to look around and see those working diligently next to us.

We bicker and fight with those we are called to love, viewing the mission and purpose God has put on our hearts to be more important than that of the other tribes.

> ***Each of you should use whatever gift you have received to serve others, as faithful stewards of God's grace in its various forms. - 1 Peter 4:10***

The gifts God has given us are not for us to use for gain but for the purpose of serving others.

List some of your spiritual gifts: Refer to 1 Corinthians 12 for a list.

Section 2:

We are first introduced to those who have a gift of apostolic anointing. They are detailed and concise, but they need the work of the other gifts to follow through with their plans.

Next, we meet those with a gift of prophetic anointing. Much like the apostles, they lead the way with vision. They can see the end from the beginning. But without the other gifts, they have no one to carry out the vision.

> **Built on the foundation of the apostles and prophets, with Christ Jesus himself as the chief cornerstone. - Ephesians 2:20**

We encounter those with the gift of evangelical anointing. They carry great zeal and fire and run with passion. But without the gifts of the others, they will burn out over time and fail without wisdom and direction.

> **But in your hearts revere Christ as Lord. Always be prepared to give an answer to everyone who asks you to give the reason for the hope that you have. But do this with gentleness and respect. - 1 Peter 3:15**

The fourth tribe is those with a gift of pastoral anointing. Strong and fearless, the pastors shepherd with kindness and compassion, doing the teaching. But without the others' gifts, they will lose the call of balance and fall prey to exhaustion.

The fifth and final tribe is those with a gift of teacher anointing. Teachers are strong leaders with a deep ambition for truth. But without the gifts of the others, they will sway in teaching and can become religious, and their zeal will burn out.

> *The Spirit of the Lord is on me, because he has anointed me to proclaim good news to the poor. He has sent me to proclaim freedom for the prisoners and recovery of sight for the blind, to set the oppressed free. - Luke 4:18*
>
> *He's after your heart. - Hosea 6:6*

Section 3:

As we study the gifts, we see there is a need for each one. But in order for the gifts to function like God created, we must learn to work together and value others' gifts.

We are living in a time when great deception is here, and the scheme of the enemy is to turn brother against brother and gift against gift. We are stronger together, and our gifts are for each other.

> *Two are better than one, because they have a good return for their labor. - Ecclesiastes 4:9*
>
> *Even so the body is not made up of one part but of many. - 1 Corinthians 12:14*
>
> *They will be divided, father against son and son against father, mother against daughter and daughter against mother, mother-in-law against daughter-in-law and daughter-in-law against mother-in-law. - Luke 12:53*

We fight against this through walking in love and finding value in the gifts that others carry.

How can you love and steward others' gifts?

Section 4:

As you encounter Kin, your longing to stay with Redeemer deepens, but you know Kin has something to teach you.

Kin begins to teach you about Paul the Apostle (you can find his story starting in Acts 7), Elijah the Prophet (you can find his story in 1 Kings 17), the woman at the well--the Evangelist (you can find her story starting in John 4), David the Shepherd (you can find his story starting in 1 Samuel 16), and John the Baptist the Teacher (you can find his story starting in the Gospels).

These are all representations of the gifts mentioned in this chapter, but Kin stops on the sixth petal and is overcome with emotion. The last one is Redeemer: He is all five and more.

"The gifts you saw with Redeemer, that is His plan for the last harvest, the training of the saints, and relationship with Him to edify the body of Christ. But they must transform under His guidance, or they will never set aside their pride and work together. Redeemer is all five. Therefore, He is the one that perfects the saints and edifies them for the work of the ministry."

> ***So Christ himself gave the apostles, the prophets, the evangelists, the pastors and teachers, to equip his people for works of service, so that the body of Christ may be built up until we all reach unity in the faith and in the knowledge of the Son of God and become mature, attaining to the whole measure of the fullness of Christ. - Ephesians 4:11-13***

Soul Expression

The gifts are Jesus's kindness to us on display, to edify the body and to transform our lives. Let your gift transform you as you enter in the refining. Be enlightened and guided. Let the real stories of the Bible be your guide as you study the gifts and allow others' gifts to bring value to your own life.

Chapter Eleven

The Cross

Section 1:

Wind blows sharply and the storm clouds form in place. Darkness surrounds you as you look for Redeemer. You pick up your shield of faith and put it in place. You sink in the mud as you walk up the ravine; every step grows heavier and more difficult under your feet. Frustration sets in as you pull yourself up from the ravine.

> ***Yes, each of you should remain as you were when God called you. - 1 Corinthians 7:20***

When it is dark and we feel lost, we can often feel like giving up; but it's His kindness that propels us forward.

God has given you the shield of faith to rely on when the wind grows too heavy. How are you using the shield of faith to protect you from the winds of life?

You use your shield to strike the ground as your leverage. I used this picture from the story in 2 Kings. When we are given instruction from the Lord, we strike the ground as an act of obedience giving us leverage to gain ground and clear the ravine.

> ***Elisha said, "Get a bow and some arrows," and he did so. "Take the bow in your hands," he said to the king of Israel. When he had taken it, Elisha put his hands on the king's hands. "Open the east window," he said, and he opened it. "Shoot!"***

Elisha said, and he shot. "The Lord's arrow of victory, the arrow of victory over Aram!" Elisha declared. "You will completely destroy the Arameans at Aphek." Then he said, "Take the arrows," and the king took them. Elisha told him, "Strike the ground." He struck it three times and stopped. The man of God was angry with him and said, "You should have struck the ground five or six times; then you would have defeated Aram and completely destroyed it. But now you will defeat it only three times." - 2 Kings 13:15-19

What does this story show you?

Ask God to show you if there is any area of your life that you are lacking obedience.

The shoes of the gospel of peace give you a boldness to move forward out of the ravine. You race through the valley towards Kin. Your armor is heavy on your body. You find a tree on top of a hill.

For to me, to live is Christ and to die is gain. - Philippians 1:21

And he said to them, "Go into all the world and proclaim the gospel to the whole creation." - Mark 16:15

Then he said to them all: "Whoever wants to be my disciple must deny themselves and take up their cross daily and follow me." - Luke 9:23

What does it mean when the Bible says "to live is Christ and to die is gain?"

Jesus has given us everything and in return we must give him everything we have. Ask God to give you a tangible way to begin the process of sharing what Christ has done for you.

Section 2:

As you reach the bottom of the hill your legs ache and your heart pounds. Thunder crashes and you fall to your knees crying out that you can't go on. Kindness reaches down and pulls you back to your feet. The Kindness of Christ propels us to keep going when we feel like we have lost all hope.

> *But when the kindness and love of God our Savior appeared, he saved us, not because of righteous things we had done, but because of his mercy. He saved us through the washing of rebirth and renewal by the Holy Spirit, whom he poured out on us generously through Jesus Christ our Savior, so that, having been justified by his grace, we might become heirs having the hope of eternal life.*
> *- Titus 3:4-7*

Do you trust the kindness of Christ?

How have you seen His Kindness in your own life?

How can you extend Christ's Kindness to others?

How can you pray for those who have hurt you instead of slandering them?

Section 3:

You reach the top of the hill and find the base of the tree. And as you look up, there you find your Redeemer nailed to the tree with blood streaming down. There is agony and pain on His face as a crown of thorns presses upon His head. His chest and eyes are whipped with deep gashes. His breathing is shallow, and you fall under the weight of anguish.

> *He was despised and rejected by mankind, a man of suffering, and familiar with pain. Like one from whom people hide their faces he was despised, and we held him in low esteem. Surely, he took up our pain and bore our suffering, yet we considered him punished by God, stricken by him, and afflicted. But he was pierced for our transgressions, he was crushed for our iniquities; the punishment that brought us peace was on him, and by his wounds we are healed. We all, like sheep, have gone astray, each of us has turned to our own way, and the Lord has laid on him the iniquity of us all. He was oppressed and afflicted, yet he did not open his mouth; he was led like a lamb to the slaughter, and as a sheep before its shearers is silent, so he did not open his mouth. By oppression and judgment, he was taken away. Yet who of his generation protested. For he was cut off from the land of the living; for the transgression of my people, he was punished. - Isaiah 53:3-8*

How does this picture of Christ on the cross make you feel?

What are your thoughts on this passage? Imagine you were there the day Christ was crucified. In your own words take a moment to picture that and write how it would make you feel.

Section 4:

As your eyes lock with His, Christ lets you know that He did this for you. He breathes His last breath and His head falls. Christ died so the veil could be torn in two and you could have access to the Father. Before the crucifixion you needed a priest to talk to God but, now that Christ died, removed sin, and rose again defeating death, you have access to God and can commune with Him. Your sin has been removed. You are covered by the blood of Jesus. The victory and power is yours.

> ***This is how God showed his love among us: He sent his one and only Son into the world that we might live through him. This is love: not that we loved God, but that he loved us and sent his Son as an atoning sacrifice for our sins. - 1 John 4:9-10***

You begin to sob under the weight of what you encountered. The words "It Is Finished" ring loudly from Redeemer.

> ***Later, knowing that everything had now been finished, and so that Scripture would be fulfilled, Jesus said, "I am thirsty." A jar of wine vinegar was there, so they soaked a sponge in it, put the sponge on a stalk of the hyssop plant, and lifted it to Jesus' lips. When he had received the drink, Jesus said, "It is finished." With that, he bowed his head and gave up his spirit. - John 19:28-30***

As you melt into the arms of Love, He comforts you with the words, "Yes, He died for you, so that the veil could be removed, and you could have the chance to stand here in my arms and in my presence. All removed, He died for you."

You are worthy because of what Jesus did for you. You are called because of Jesus. You can come boldly to the throne of grace and find the arms of Love. He will tell you of things to come and be your guide and source because of Jesus.

> *Let us then approach God's throne of grace with confidence, so that we may receive mercy and find grace to help us in our time of need. - Hebrews 4:16*

> *How great is your goodness, which you have stored up for those who fear you, which you bestow in the sight of men on those who take refuge in you. - Psalm 31:19*

God calls you worthy and chosen because of the price that Jesus paid for you. Proclaim your righteousness through the power of Christ.

How has your life changed because of Jesus?

You see Redeemer in the distance alive and well. You run to Him with Wind propelling you forward. He has risen; His life would not be condemned to a tomb. Christ defeated death and He lives.

> *He is not here; he has risen! Remember how he told you, while he was still with you in Galilee: 'The Son of Man must be delivered over to the hands of sinners, be crucified and on the third day be raised again. - Luke 24:6-7*

> *For we know that since Christ was raised from the dead, he cannot die again; death no longer has mastery over him. - Romans 6:9*

Not only did Christ defeat sin and bring healing, but He also defeated death. His power has the final say. True healing comes from locking eyes with the fire. Allow Jesus to come and encounter you with truth. Lock eyes with Jesus's Fire-Filled ones, what do you see?

Section 5:

You watch as Love embraces Redeemer knowing the Father is well pleased with His Son. You turn to meet Kindness. You realize the purpose of seeing the crucifixion was Christ's Kindness as you step into the fullness of truth.

> *And a voice from heaven said, "This is my Son, whom I love; with him I am well pleased." - Matthew 3:17*

You watch as Redeemer and Love converse with the friends you have met along your journey. Each of these friends represent a character of God.

> *But the fruit of the Spirit is love, joy, peace, forbearance, kindness, goodness, faithfulness, gentleness and self-control. Against such things is no law. - Galatians 5:22-23*

Redeemer turns to you and says, "You are Chosen." This is your identity; this is your victory; this is who you are.

> *You did not choose me, but I chose you and appointed you so that you might go and bear fruit—fruit that will last—and so that whatever you ask in my name the Father will give you. - John 15:16*

In closing, let us turn to the Redeemer of our soul. We are called and chosen for such a time as this. Jesus is our example, our forerunner, and the perfecter of our faith. Let us turn to Him as the example in our lives. May His words and teaching take root in our hearts and propel us into the destiny that has been laid out before us. You are chosen, you are worthy, you are wanted. Walk in the assurance of your new identity found and hidden in Christ Jesus. Let us not look back to our past but allow the promise, goodness, and kindness of Christ to be our guide in the future as we take back territory for the Kingdom of God. Do not look to the left or the right but keep your eyes locked with Him as He opens doors. Take His hand; journey with Him. He is your safe place. He is your source. He is worth all that we have because He already gave it all so you could walk boldly into the throne of grace.

Coming Soon...

Valued

Hello, my friend, I have been with you the entire time. I'm the breeze across your face. I'm the fire in Loved and Redeemers eyes. I'm the encouragement in your step. I hover over the earth and dwell within the heart of man. I was in the beginning; I'm in the middle and I will be there in the end. I'm not confined by time, and boundless in love and energy. I lack nothing, I Am wisdom, encouragement, and counselor. I flourish best when I'm unboxed and free to move.

I know the will of God and the heart of Jesus. I Am the communicator sent on your behalf to journey alongside of you. I came to set the world ablaze. To encourage sons and daughters of God to step out as a flame to reach the world. I came to convict those who have yet to give their life to Jesus, to show them his endless power and the great depth of freedom He has for them. I Am a picture of the Spirit of God. I lack nothing, I Am not conformed to a body, and I Am able to move through dimensions. I have come to give you wisdom and comfort. This world can be cruel and confusing with every twist and turn bringing another distraction.

With me you will not grow weary or lack joy. I will refresh your Spirit with my beauty and my nature. I'm not of this world and do things in my own time. I hear the voice of the Father because I Am one with Him and I will remind you of the words He speaks. Through acceptance of me, you will discover what it means to bring value to a world on fire. The world is so focused on self-pleasing tactics, but I'm focused on a heart that gives bountifully. A heart that loves his enemy and desires to obey the Father's heart.

Moving forward, I ask that you remove your preconceived ideas of me. Others may have theories of who I Am, but I will not be boxed in by theories. Whatever you desire to know of me, simply ask. I Am the wind in the scriptures, the color in the rainbow and the joy in laughter. I Am also the thunder in the storm and the fear in the presence of God

I'm neither male nor female, I'm simply Spirit and truth. I can embody whoever and whatever the Father wills. I'm clever, creative, and patient. I desire to bring your eternal desire back as you learn to glow in my fire. You have value to bring to this world through your dreams and purpose. I will teach you how to align your will with the will of the Father.

This life is not your own, by welcoming me in, I will change your perspective on everything. I will set you free, I will walk with you, I will never leave you. I Am who I Am. You are like a city on a hill; I Am the light within the city. Let me light you up and send you out for such a time as this.

Let's continue the journey that you finished with Redeemer. In my presence there is a union of richness to be explored. Together, let's take what we have learned along the way and embrace what Love and Redeemer have taught us. New Friends await. The remainder of our armor awaits. Your freedom on the file leg of the journey awaits.

Grab my hand, let's go!

ABOUT KHARIS PUBLISHING

KHARIS PUBLISHING is an independent, traditional publishing house with a core mission to publish impactful books, and channel proceeds into establishing mini-libraries or resource centers for orphanages in developing countries, so these kids will learn to read, dream, and grow. Every time you purchase a book from Kharis Publishing or partner as an author, you are helping give these kids an amazing opportunity to read, dream, and grow. Kharis Publishing is an imprint of Kharis Media LLC. Learn more at https://www.kharispublishing.com.

www.ingramcontent.com/pod-product-compliance
Lightning Source LLC
Chambersburg PA
CBHW070158100426
42743CB00013B/2964